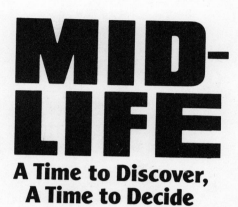

MID-LIFE

**A Time to Discover,
A Time to Decide**

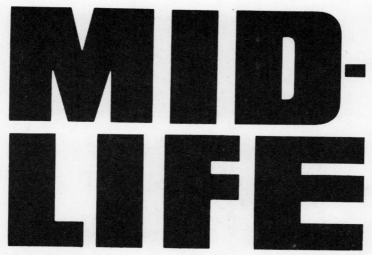

MID-LIFE

A Time to Discover, A Time to Decide

A Christian Perspective on Middle Age

Richard P. Olson

Judson Press ® Valley Forge

Mid-Life: A Time to Discover, a Time to Decide

Copyright © 1980
Judson Press, Valley Forge, PA 19481

Library of Congress Cataloging in Publication Data
Olson, Richard P.
  Mid-life, a time to discover, a time to decide.

  Includes bibliographical references and index.
  1. Middle age—United States. 2. Age and employment—United States. 3. Maturation (Psychology)
I. Title.
HQ 1059.5.U5057   305.2'4   80-10709
ISBN 0-8170-0859-4

ACKNOWLEDGMENTS

In addition to those authors and publishers whose contributions I have noted in the time-honored way of notes and permission fees, I would like to acknowledge the help of many people.

My appreciation to groups on middle age—both in First Baptist Church, Racine, Wisconsin, and at the National Christian Education Conference at Green Lake, Wisconsin—where experiences were shared, questions were raised, and the fellowship of the pilgrimage was experienced.

My thanks to Charles Oehrig, Department of Ministry with Adults, American Baptist Educational Ministries, for hearing me out on this concern and authorizing my preparing of three articles, which formed the seed for this book.

I am appreciative that Charles Oehrig and Wayne Johnson read parts of the manuscript and offered most helpful and perceptive criticisms.

My gratitude to Judson Press editors Harold Twiss and Phyllis Frantz for conscientious, thorough editing. Through their efforts, the number of meaningless, meandering sentences herein has been significantly reduced.

Many thanks to Ron Brinkmann and to the Wayland Community

who provided me places where for a few hours or a few days I could meditate and write without interruption.

I am grateful to Becky Lannon for her visual impressions that are included on the first page of each chapter.

A special thanks to Virginia Pipe. I met her in June; and in August, we co-led a consultation on mid-life together. In the weeks in between she unselfishly served as consultant, critic, encourager, and contributor to this project over the miles from Colorado to Wisconsin. I particularly appreciate her perspective on women's issues in middle age. Ginny, whatever this book is, it is better than it would have been without you.

Finally, thanks to daughter Julie Olson for research assistance and typing on the final draft; and to wife Mary Ann Olson for typing on the final draft. How reassuring it was to see neat, attractive pages arising out of my shambles of composed, reconsidered, re-edited pages! It was good to see the promise of orderliness and meaning to this project. Sorry it came on so fast so late, gals. Praises be! My family survived the tensions of this project intact.

TABLE OF CONTENTS

1

MY STRANGE, PREDICTABLE DIS-EASE

Mid-Life Experienced

As one who feels he is relatively self-aware, I was shocked at my response to my fortieth birthday. Though my logical brain said, "I've been aging all my life, and one birthday isn't much different from another," something deep within my emotions did not agree. A perceptive thirty-nine-year-old had once noted, "Next birthday, I'll be ten years older." That was just how I felt. I began to understand why Jack Benny had gotten so much laugh mileage out of "being thirty-nine." He did so because turning forty rubs a universal raw nerve. That nerve in me was being painfully rubbed!

Several troubling themes began to float intertwined through my emotional life. One theme was a disappointment with myself, my career, my achievements. I had held some fond dreams about the direction my career would take. As a matter of fact, I had gone back to school to pick up the credentials to be ready for that dreamed-about turn in my career. But very few doors of opportunity had opened to me, and then ever so slightly. Then the doors shut rather suddenly. As I unsuccessfully tried to elbow my way into a crowded field (a specialized part of higher education), I received "turn downs." When I was younger, I could shrug off these rejections with the thought of "some day." After the age of forty when a rejection notice came, it seemed to say, "Never!" Never would I get the chance to have exactly the career I wanted. Frustration and bitterness were constant temptations. Not infrequently, the temptation won, at least for a time.

Another theme was concern about my own body. I had always enjoyed vigorous health. I had assumed I could do more than others because I needed less sleep. But now, things seemed to change drastically and quite suddenly. Did I tire more easily? Need more sleep? Have less endurance for a vigorous physical game? Ache more after strenuous exercise? It seemed so. Was that long-ignored flutter in my chest the early warning of a heart attack, so common to us middle-aged men?

I still don't know whether such changes were the result of changing physiology or whether my psyche was playing tricks on my body. However, one incident did make clear that my body was indeed changing. My eye examination revealed the need for bifocals. I took the prescription with this disappointing news to my optician, a friend older than I. He looked at the prescription and asked, "How old are you, Dick?" "Forty-two," I replied. He responded, "You're right on schedule!"

But by far the most troubling theme for me was *time* (or more accurately the lack of and shortness of time) and *death*. For several months after my fortieth birthday, I either dreamt about death every night or else the first thought that occurred to me upon waking was, "It's too bad about death." Gradually the dreams decreased, but the dread remained. This preoccupation-dread was particularly troubling to me since I thought I had appropriated the gospel's perspective on death. Indeed, I had comforted and consoled many persons with that gospel. But what I had offered to others, I seemingly had not adequately grasped for myself. I believe it was Luther who once said that everyone must do one's own believing and one's own dying. I was discovering the truth of what he said. Since I was regularly called to minister when persons in my congregation died, I could not entirely ignore or repress the subject of death, as do so many other mid-lifers.

Equally pressing was the feeling that time was closing in upon me, that a lifetime would not be adequate to achieve my aspirations. Daily-weekly-monthly time gave precious few moments to find enjoyment or fulfillment. Of course, this was the result of the workaholic life-style I had created. But though that life-style no longer made sense to me, it seemed to be an addiction too strong to break. Therefore, rather than renegotiating a more appropriate work schedule, I engaged in self-pity or resentment when time demands seemed overwhelming.

Coupled with all this was a feeling that this life crisis was absolutely unique, unlike anything before it in my experience (largely true) and that I was utterly alone in it (not true, but more about that later).

I was fortunate that my mid-life struggle was relatively mild. Very rarely did my inner turmoil interfere with my fulfilling my responsibilities. For the most part, I kept on as if nothing unusual were going on inside—although I don't suppose my preaching had much joy in it those two years. But much of the time, the secret inner pain was nearly overwhelming.

With the help of some resources I will shortly describe, the worst part passed and I came to a relative calm and peace about these matters. And so, when my wife, Mary Ann, reached her fortieth birthday, I felt ready to help her through the wilderness.

"How does it feel to be forty, dear?" I asked her. "Nothing special or unusual," she replied. Unsatisfied, I probed, "But don't you feel time closing in on you?" "No," she responded. "With the children growing older, I feel I am going to have more time to do the things I want. I feel time opening up to me."

Talks with women friends showed me that many shared Mary Ann's feelings. One told me, "Middle age came to me when I sensed my two sons were grown up. I felt so unneeded—and so open to countless possibilities. It was like beginning life again!"

While no generalizations absolutely apply, observers note that many females do experience middle age much differently from many males. Males may sense a limitation of time; females, an expansion of time. Men may want to cut down on career aspirations while women may be becoming increasingly excited about career development. Males may become more interested in their emotional, introspective side, while females may be discovering their competitive, assertive side. Men may be becoming increasingly more home-oriented at a time when women are becoming less so. Men may be experiencing a diminished or uncertain sex drive at the same time women are experiencing a greater sexual awareness. Men may be encountering more despair at a time when women are experiencing more hope. A more detailed description of one woman's experience is on page 14.

But, back to my story. Some observers feel that the crisis I experienced is mostly a function of time, a developmental stage of life. They term it a "mid-life crisis." It is the initiation to "middle adulthood," or "middle age." They contend, further, that just as time brought the problem on, time will take it away. "Just sit there and do nothing" they advise.

There is a kernel of truth in that statement, but I fear the kernel makes it into a dangerous half-truth. For though some experience relief without taking any action, it is doubtful they learn anything from the experience. On the other hand, this crisis can be a rich opportunity for personal awareness and growth.

It proved to be just that growth opportunity for me. For in the pain and uneasiness of this crisis I blundered into four ways of dealing with it. Let me tell you about these methods.

a. I read. When my fortieth birthday hit, I was unaware that there was a literature for us "middlescents." But one day while I was in the library, I happened on a full shelf of such books. I was amazed when I began reading experiences so similar to mine that I could have written them myself. These authors faced the dark experiences of which I spoke and then moved on to hope (though in most of these books it was a secular hope). The companionship of those books was a great comfort.

b. I communicated with close friends. I am fortunate to have two close male friends whose birthdays are within months of mine. Frequently, during those years, we compared notes. Because we live some distances from each other, the telephone company grew richer during my season of adversity.

c. I convened a group of middle-aged persons in my church in response to the request of a parishioner. We sent out invitations and a lively group responded. I honestly told them that I would partly be solving my problem by helping them work on theirs. As one man told me near the conclusion of our group, "I'm not sure I've found any answers, but at least now I don't feel so alone with my questions." He had expressed my sentiments as well.

d. I spent a good deal of time in personal meditation and reflection. I searched for my own worth and significance as a person. I looked for the affirmation that what I did mattered even if all my dreams would not be fulfilled. I assessed past and future relationally with regard to self, family, congregation, friends, and God. I pondered what Christian growth and maturity would look like. While I've always known I am a person with a need for periods of privacy and solitude, these needs became vitally important to me in this period of life.

These activities did help me work through the crisis with more than a little insight and provided an uncommonly fertile medium for growth. If you are reading this book out of personal need rather than casual interest, I urge the same four ways of dealing with your mid-life crises for you. And I will give you help.

If you are one who gains insight through *reading,* there is rich literature available to you and I will point it out to you. Many of the more significant works on middle age have appeared since I first started reading in this field.

I urge you to reclaim old *friends* or work hard at establishing new ones with whom you can be transparent about your inner world. I am constantly saddened to find how few people have persons they can call "buddy" or "pal." But such persons—the kind you can call any time to tell anything, no matter how petty, gloomy, or sordid—are a valuable resource for the joy of living.

I further urge you to find persons of similar age and concern in your church. You might even call them together to discuss *this* book. Help yourself by helping others to be in touch with your life stories and the emotions and decisions you now face.

And I invite you into the discipline of contemplation-meditation. I hope this book will provide a broad perspective that can serve as the point of departure for your inner reckoning.

The next chapter contains an overview of life stages, summarizing recent research and writing in this field. Then in succeeding chapters, I will examine certain important middle adult issues with you. I will do this not simply as an amateur psychologist but as a person of faith. I believe that there are certain biblical-theological themes that speak particularly to us as middle-aged persons. And I believe that because of our stage in life we can understand and relate to these themes better than when we were younger. Rich spiritual discovery awaits us. In the final chapter, I will put these biblical insights together into a preliminary theology of middle age.

I make no claim to have arrived, but am eager to share with you as a fellow struggler. As will be obvious to you, I feel more comfortable with some of the subjects we will explore than with others. I eagerly anticipate writing some chapters, but dread writing others. Since I try not to play games with myself, writing those difficult chapters will provide a new occasion for self-exploration and growth.

My hope is that you will explore the book, benefit from it, challenge it when it does not fit you, and eventually outgrow it.

Peace and joy to you as we share this part of our pilgrimage together!

P.S. Mid-Life Crisis in a Woman's Experience

After I had written this chapter, Virginia Pipe shared with me the story of her mid-life crisis. I was so touched that I asked her to share it with you and she graciously agreed,—Virginia?

As I sit here in the quiet early morning hours, I am tempted to set aside until some other time the recounting and recalling of the first painful year spent here in Grand Junction, Colorado, when I was age forty-one. The fact of being forty-one was not bothersome, because at age thirty-eight I had congratulated myself on finally getting it fairly together after having spent twenty-five years of resisting being female and feeling cheated by my inadequate, pathetic father. Enough of the Freudian jazz!

The fact remains that, within the last two years of living in Royal Oak, Michigan, I had decided to go back to school and thus had gone through the frightening ten-stage process of registering for post-degree courses at Wayne State University in a field house with ten thousand other people. I had come within a whisker of panicking and bolting for the entrance, but I took myself in hand, as I had done when my first child was due, and said to myself, "If all those other people can make it through, I can do it, too." After all, I thought, I ought to be able to figure out how to get from Station A to Station J. However, my gut was churning, my head aching, and my psyche in shock. Although I didn't realize it that day, I came to realize later that the worst of reentering the world of education was over. Registration was more scary than the courses.

I loved the class work, and spent a year cramming in psych courses and getting the required Statistics course done so that I could apply for graduate school in Clinical Psychology. I wasn't even too discouraged when I learned that in order to take the Stat course I had to take two other math courses—an algebra refresher to bring back those twenty-five-year-old learnings from Mr. Snyder and a trigonometry course, which was almost totally unrelated, but someone had figured that if you could hack trig you could pass stat.

Finally I was at the completion of this year of undergraduate studies and in the process of applying for and being rejected by several grad programs. One rejection was a very clearly discriminatory one because the head honcho wanted "budding *young* geniuses" who could undividedly pursue a Ph.D. in Clinical Psych without family encumbrances. My four children at that time were nine, ten, eleven, and fourteen.

About that time, my husband was called to an administrative church position in Colorado, with the stipulation that we live on the Western Slope. What I didn't fully realize until arriving in Grand Junction was that it would be impossible for me to pursue a graduate degree without going "over the hill" in some direction—west or east 250 or so miles to Salt Lake City or Denver or south to Gunnison or Alamosa—to do the resident work required for a graduate degree.

I struggled bravely for over a year, slowly going downhill despite being heavily involved in church and other volunteer work. Then, in the fall of 1973, the roof caved in, the bottom fell out, and I sank into a depression so profound that I wanted desperately to die. I was frightened, and so was my husband, of the prospect of starting on the long road of manic-depression which afflicted my father from age forty-five until his death at sixty-seven. I had just turned forty-two.

I won't say more about the depressive episode because I'd frankly rather not dwell on it, but it was the bottoming out. From that point to this there has been fairly steady progress. I became deeply involved in the start-up of a Women's Resource Center. I accidentally stumbled upon a graduate program in adult education which required five weeks on campus and essentially was self-directed learning. Thank God for Jim Kincaid, my faculty adviser who made this flexible learning program possible. I plugged away for four years, receiving my M.Ed. from Colorado State University. My final project was the designing, field testing, and evaluation of an eight-week, twenty-four-hour small group experience for homemakers who were approaching or in the empty nest. Another woman who shared my struggles and I formed a consulting business, operating from our homes and offering classes mostly through the Women's Resource Center. After a year at that venture, in January, 1979, we joined with three therapists to purchase a house and form a collective called the Family Counseling and Learning Center. My partner and I are the Learning Center component of the business.

What I need to say to you and what I kept repeating to myself many times during this period when I was scared or discouraged was, "What's the alternative?" For me, the frightening alternative was long-term mild-to-severe depression and limited functioning. The prospect of a psychotic episode, which I felt had been very close at one point of immobilization, was sometimes the only thing that kept me moving forward despite fear and trembling. Somehow at this point I knew the choice was between life and death—not physical, but psychological and spiritual death—and I chose *life*.[1]

Do You Qualify?

By the time you've reached middle age, you have likely come to the conclusion that most psychological self-tests are frauds, prepared for the credulous by the unaccredited.

This is true of the following quiz, but perhaps it beats astrology. And, like the compulsive gambler, you may decide a fixed game is better than none at all.

So—kindly grab a pencil, adjust your bubble gum/bifocals/heating pad/ and begin.

Please mark the following questions true or false:

1. ___ Your wife now insists on shoveling snow for you.
2. ___ You notice that the airlines are permitting much younger girls to serve as stewardesses.
3. ___ You call airline hostesses "stewardesses."
4. ___ Friday night is the beginning of the weekend.
5. ___ Friday night is the end of the week.
6. ___ All your friends are getting fat, and look tired.
7. ___ You have observed that washroom attendants don't smile as much as they used to, even when you give them the dime.
8. ___ Clothing sizes are getting smaller, winters colder, popular songs stupider.
9. ___ You can recall when it was possible to make out the words of a popular song.
10. ___ You can remember when hoods were called gangsters and were chased by G-men.
11. ___ A good way to read fine print is hold it farther away.
12. ___ Your doctor has told you not to eat *any* of your favorite foods.

Now for some multiple choice: If stranded on a desert island, your ultimate wish (except rescue) would be:

a. *a companion of the opposite sex*
b. *a kit of boat-building tools*
c. *a suitable memorial*

Miniskirts remind you of:

a. *sex*
b. *chilblains*
c. *your granddaughter*

At your job, the majority of your time is spent:

a. *kidding the secretaries/men*
b. *working*
c. *figuring out your pension*

"Plates" are:
a. *wedding gifts*
b. *uppers and lowers*
You have just joined a gym; your purpose is:
a. *to get out of the house one night a week*
b. *to prevent a heart attack*
A drive-in movie is:
a. *a way to avoid paying a baby-sitter*
b. *full of mosquitoes*
c. *for kids*
Tom Wolfe is the author of:
a. *The Electric Kool-Aid Acid Test*
b. *Look Homeward, Angel*
"Blood, Sweat, and Tears" is:
a. *a popular rock group*
b. *a phrase from Churchill*
"Peace" is:
a. *something to fight for*
b. *a controversial word*
c. *a rocking chair*
A rumble seat is:
a. *a rare disease*
b. *fun for two*
c. *temptation for youth*
Friends you haven't seen for years tell you:
a. *You've changed so much!*
b. *You haven't changed a bit!*
c. *You look wonderful!*

If you marked mostly "false" and "**a**" you should read this book to understand your elders; if you chose mostly "**c**," you should peruse it to understand your middle-aged offspring.

But, if you answered "true" to nearly all but number 4 of the first list of questions, and checked "**b**" on most of the multiple choice, you're a perfect middle-ager.*

*Elliott McCleary, "Do You Qualify?" from "Generation in the Middle," *Blue Print for Health*, vol. 23, no. 1 (1970), pp. 24-25. Published by the Blue Cross Association, 840 Lake Shore Drive, Chicago, IL 60611. Reprinted with permission from "Generation in the Middle," published by the Blue Cross Association.

2
SEASONS, PASSAGES, AND TRANSFORMATIONS
The Discovery of Middle Age

"We unfold and grow; we have fallow periods and seasons of sudden spurts of change; we are not the same today as we were yesterday, and we will have gone, before we age, through at least three or four distinctively different growth periods."[1]

Indulge me for a moment and engage in a playful metaphor. Imagine for a moment that all of human life is one huge circus under an enormous tent. Imagine that all the behavioral scientists (psychologists, sociologists, etc.,) are the observers of the show.

If you can imagine this, you will notice something strange. Those observers are concentrated in two places. A large crowd of them is gathered by the entrance, observing childhood and adolescence. A somewhat smaller crowd is gathered at the exit observing aging, senility, and dying. But, concludes the creator of this metaphor, Bernice Neugarten, "Both groups really have been missing the main show—that is, what's going on in the three-ring circus that we call adulthood."[2]

Perhaps students of personality have ignored these middle adult years because they accepted the myth that adults are fully developed, static, unchanging, and, therefore, extremely boring subjects to study. Possibly they bought the assumption in the old fairy tales that

19

the exciting part of the story is the part in which the handsome young prince and the youthful, poor but beautiful, maiden conquer all obstacles that would keep them apart. The story always concludes, "And they married and lived happily ever after." Says who? Don't you wish life were that easy? On the other hand, if it were, wouldn't life be dull? The assumption that needs to be challenged is, "While children change, adults only age."[3]

Fortunately, there is a developing viewpoint of what it means to be an adult. There are even some new terms being coined. One may now use the term "middlescence" to suggest a period of life just as "adolescence" refers to a period of life. One writer speaks of "mediatrics," the study of adults in the middle of life, similar to "geriatrics," the study of adults near the end of life.

Much fruitful study has recently been conducted on the life stages in general and the middle years of adulthood in particular. I will present briefly the views of several of these scholars who describe life stages and middle years from slightly different perspectives. Their insights will inform our discussion for the rest of the book.

Erik Erikson, The Eight Stages of a Person

Erik Erikson has stated the concept that there are eight stages in the life cycle of a person. The first four of these occur during infancy and childhood as follows:

1. *Infancy: Trust versus mistrust.* During this period the task for the person is to develop a basic sense of trust in oneself, in others, in the environment. This comes primarily through the quality of care received in those years.

2. *Early Childhood: Autonomy versus shame and doubt.* As the child grows, one experiments with holding on and letting go; in short, the development of autonomous will occurs during this stage. The task is to learn to use this will without shame and doubt.

3. *Play Age: Initiative versus guilt.* The child is able to move about freely, communicate, express curiosity, have fantasies. One also begins to experience conscience.

4. *School Age: Industry versus inferiority.* The child learns how to do and make things with others. One either receives recognition and encouragement in these efforts or experiences a sense of inferiority if the recognition does not come.

After these four stages that occur in childhood, Erikson observes four additional stages that occur in teen and adult years.

5. *Adolescence: Identity versus role confusion.* As the person experiences rapid body growth, maturing sexuality, and a gradual approach to adult responsibilities, his or her task is to integrate these new experiences into a new identity. This new identity has continuity with the identity one felt as a child but has elements of newness and becoming as well. However, unless the old identity and the new identity are fully integrated, one is not ready for the next stages of life.

6. *Young Adulthood: Intimacy versus isolation.* As one becomes more secure in one's own identity, the next task is to establish intimacy with one's inner self and with others, both in friendships and in a love-based, mutually satisfying sexual relationship.

7. *Adulthood: Generativity versus stagnation.* When one has been able to establish intimacies in adulthood, the next issue is *generativity;* that is, the mature person's interest in establishing and guiding the next generation. This is a commitment to and caring about the next generation. The person unable to do this may experience a sense of stagnation and impoverishment both within oneself and in relationships.

8. *Later Adulthood: Ego integrity versus despair.* The task is to reach the end of life with ego integrity—acceptance of responsibility for one's life, belief that one's life has had meaning and purpose. Quite obviously, to fail to achieve this is to fall into despair.[4]

Erikson has pointed out what the basic issues are that one must face to live effectively. However, in my opinion, they do not fall quite as neatly into life stages as the above outline might imply. Granted there are stages in life when the life tasks he describes may be of utmost importance. Still, I find myself as a middle-ager wrestling with at least the last four of those stages much of the time.

Identity: As a middle-ager, my body, my sexuality, my role in society, and my family status are changing, and with these changes I ask with new urgency, "Who am I?"

Intimacy: For the last nineteen years, most of my intimacy has been work, marriage, or child oriented. Spare time was devoted to effective parenthood. But now, my teenage children need me less. I find myself looking for skills, initiative, and a new dose of risk-taking to establish new relationships to take the place of those I am gradually losing.

Generativity: Yes, indeed! I am hoping my children and those with whom I work will reflect what I have tried to model, counsel, and teach. I worry about the boredom, cynicism, and "broken-record" criticism that creeps into my outlook from time to time.

Integrity: Maybe I'm an early worrier, but I am very conscious of my mortality and someday death. The meaningfulness and integrity of my life are most important to me. How I hope my life has some lasting significance!

Further, these life issues are never neatly resolved. I suspect I'm a little generative and slightly stagnant, a bit hopeful of integrity, and somewhat despairing about my life! Life stages are not quite as concise as Erikson's outline makes them appear. His greatest insight is that *growth and development take place over a person's entire lifetime.*

Further, some have suggested that three of the life issues and life stages that Erikson describes occur in a different sequence for *men* than for *women.* They might be charted as follows.

	Men's Issues	Women's Issues
Adolescence	*Identity* (Who am I?)	*Intimacy* (To whom and in what manner do I relate?)
Young Adult	*Intimacy* (To whom and in what manner do I relate?)	*Generativity* (How do I bear and influence my children in a meaningful way?)
Adulthood	*Generativity* (How do I influence my children and other children?)	*Identity* (Who am I?)

But perhaps these sequences are not quite right either. William Bridges points out that there are two ways of reflecting on human development. One way of viewing development is by seeing it as being naturally sequential, linear, purposive, one developmental state occurring at a time. (Call this the masculine way of looking at things or the yang path.) The other is to view development in a much more holistic and intuitive manner. (Call this the feminine way of looking at things or the yin path.)

Bridges suggests that these two ways of looking at development may be contrasted by the image of the chain and the braid. The chain is a figure which represents the method of seeing each developmental period in logical, sequential order—first link: identity; second link: intimacy; third link: generativity, etc. The braid is a quite different image. Instead of solid separate links, there are continuous flexible strands. When you view development as a chain, a cross section at any given moment reveals one link as basic. There is some central task with which one must deal. When you view development as a braid, a cross section at any given age reveals that all the strands are present. One is holistically dealing with identity *and* intimacy *and* generativity.[5] And this may be more expressive of women's experiences of life stages: not a sequence of tasks, but a developing intuitive reaction with several life tasks in concert with each other.

Daniel Levinson, The Seasons of a Man's Life

Daniel J. Levinson and associates have investigated the stages of life from a different perspective. Where Erikson concentrated on unconscious processes in the development of adult identity, Levinson explored the conscious choices a man makes regarding his occupation, marriage, family, friends, and life goals.

Levinson and his colleagues did intensive interviews with forty men. Regretfully they did not also interview women to compare their life stages. The forty men were equally divided among four occupations: industrial laborers, biology professors, business executives, and novelists. Out of these interviews came a concept of life stages that is expressed in their recently published work, *The Seasons of a Man's Life*.[6]

Levinson believes that the life cycle evolves through a series of eras, each of them approximately twenty-five years in duration. The sequence is as follows:

1. Childhood and adolescence: age 0-22
2. Early adulthood: age 17-45
3. Middle adulthood: age 40-65
4. Late adulthood: age 60-?[7]

"Each era has its own distinctive and unifying qualities," like the act of a play or the major section of a novel. Of course, change and development do take place within each era.

One of Levinson's surprises was that development in adult years is age-linked.[8] While not everyone develops along exactly the same time sequence, he found the age variations for the different eras did not vary by more than five or six years.

He concludes then that there is a *clearly identifiable, studyable progression of development for adults, just as there is for children and youth.*

On the border between each of the life stages, Levinson discovered that there is a "zone of overlap." That is the period when the old era is being completed and the new one is starting. This is not a simple, brief transition. It is rather the change of the fabric of one's life. Such transitions consistently take four or five years. The person's task in this time is to do the developmental work that links the eras and provides some continuity between them.

In broad outline, then, this is how Levinson diagrams the eras of a man's life:

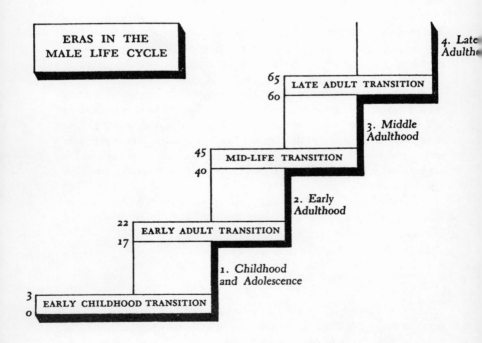

Daniel J. Levinson, Charlotte N. Darrow, Edward B. Klein, Maria H. Levinson, Braxton McKee, *The Seasons of a Man's Life* (New York: Alfred A. Knopf, Inc., 1978), p. 20.

Of course, this chart describes a person's life in broad strokes. There is much change and development within each era. Therefore, his more delicate analysis of the early and middle adult eras looks something like this.

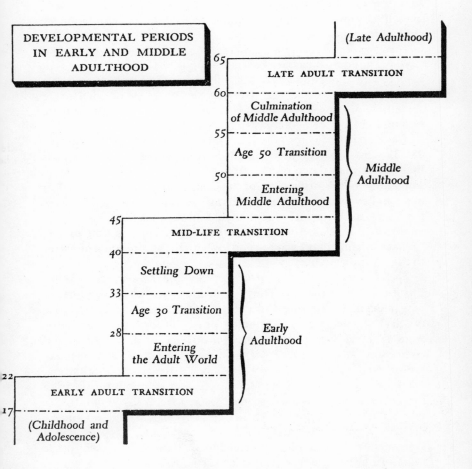

DEVELOPMENTAL PERIODS IN EARLY AND MIDDLE ADULTHOOD

(Late Adulthood)

65

LATE ADULT TRANSITION

60

Culmination of Middle Adulthood

55

Age 50 Transition

50

Entering Middle Adulthood

Middle Adulthood

45

MID-LIFE TRANSITION

40

Settling Down

33

Age 30 Transition

28

Entering the Adult World

Early Adulthood

22

EARLY ADULT TRANSITION

17

(Childhood and Adolescence)

Daniel J. Levinson, Charlotte N. Darrow, Edward B. Klein, Maria H. Levinson, Braxton McKee, *The Seasons of a Man's Life* (New York: Alfred A. Knopf, Inc., 1978), p. 57.

The basic development tasks of each of these periods of adult development (to age 50) are outlined below.[9]

Early Adult Transition: Moving from Pre- to Early Adulthood (ages 17–22). There are two tasks in this period. One is to start moving out of the pre-adult world, and the second is to make a preliminary step into the adult world. One must explore possibilities, imagine oneself as a participant in the adult world, and make preliminary choices for adult living.

The First Adult Structure: Entering the Adult World (ages 22–28). A young adult man has two basic, yet opposite, tasks: (*a*) he needs to explore all the possibilities of adult living; and (*b*) he needs to settle down, create a stable life structure: become responsible, make something of himself. He must also find some balance between these two tasks of exploring and settling.

The Age Thirty Transition: Changing the First Life Structure (ages 28–33). This five-year period provides opportunity to work on the limitations and flaws of the first adult structure and to create something more satisfactory for the balance of early adulthood. For many in Levinson's study, there was an age thirty crisis—a time when the man finds his present life structure intolerable, yet finds himself unable to formulate something better. This crisis is a time to ask, "What's missing that I want to add? What's inappropriate that I want to take out of my life?"

The Second Adult Life Structure: Settling Down (ages 33–40). From the end of the Age Thirty Transition until about age forty, a person enters the settling down period of his life calendar. There are two tasks in this period: (*a*) finding a niche in society and changing from a "novice" adult to one more firmly accepted, respected, and competent; and (*b*) making it, advancing in social rank, income, power, fame, creativity, quality of family life, social contribution, etc.

At the end of the Settling Down period, from about thirty-six to forty, Levinson notes a distinctive phase he calls *Becoming One's Own Man* (or, as he abbreviates it, BOOM!). The major developmental task here is to become a senior member in one's world with a greater measure of authority. The added responsibility means that more of one's "little boy" has to be surrendered.

The Mid-Life Transition: Moving from Early to Middle Adulthood (ages 40–45). In this transition period, the life structure again comes into question. One asks:

What have I done with my life? What do I really get from and give to my wife, children, friends, work, community—and self? What is it I truly want for myself and others? What are my central values and how are they reflected in my life? What are my greatest talents and how am I using (or wasting) them? What have I done with my early Dream and what do I want with it now? Can I live in a way that combines my current desires, values and talents? How satisfactory is my present life structure—how suitable for the self, how viable in the world—and how shall I change it to provide a better basis for the future? [10]

For 80 percent of the men they interviewed, this transition was a time of moderate or severe crisis. Nearly every aspect of one's life comes under scrutiny and questioning. A person will need several years to build a new path or modify an old one.

Entering Middle Adulthood: Building a New Life Structure (ages 45–50). The man must now make his choices and begin forming a new life structure. Levinson notes that men vary greatly in the success-appropriateness of the life structure they build at this time. Those who build a success-appropriate life structure are the ones who most successfully build a structure that is reasonably viable in the world and connected to the self they have discovered in this searching process. [11]

He points out that there are *three aspects* of the developmental work of early and middle adulthood. [12]

The *first* aspect is *building* and *modifying* the *life structure*. In a stable period, one's basic task is to build a life structure and enhance one's life within it. In those transitions between stable periods, one must terminate the existing structure, explore possibilities (both inner and outer), and make new choices.

The second aspect is *working on single components* of the *Life Structure*. Levinson notes five components that have special importance in the individual's growth and development: (*a*) Forming and Modifying a Dream. In early adulthood a man needs to form a dream (relationally and occupationally) and then to attain goals in which he in some measure fulfills the dream. "In middle adulthood, his task is to modify or give up the Dream." (*b*) Forming and Modifying an Occupation. Some stay in a single occupation, but most make a few or many changes. Even if one stays in the same broadly defined occupation, he will make many subtle changes, such as work place, status, identity, or difficulty of work. (*c*) Love-Marriage-Family. The men in the study went through considerable variation in their interest, skill, and self-investment in forming and maintaining marriage and family relationships. In many cases, interest in family increased with the middle years. (*d*) Forming Mentoring Relationships. Levinson uses the term "mentor" to describe one who is a teacher, a model, an influence on a person's life, an "admixture of good father and good friend."[13] There is an era in one's life when one needs mentoring. But then the mentor must be let go. Eventually there comes a time when one is willing to be mentor to younger, aspiring co-workers or to one's own children. (*e*) Forming Mutual Friendships. Levinson found that the men he studied had few male friends and even fewer nonsexual female friendships.

The third task is *adult individuation,* that is, the task of discovering "who I am in a unique sense." Backed by all the experience of living and all the life tasks the man has already accomplished, he raises the question of his unique identity once more with more depth. He needs to discover himself in relationship to himself, to others, and to the exterior world. Levinson feels that one achieves this individuation by dealing with four polarities or opposite forces that are occurring in one's life. The four polarities are the following:

1. Young/Old. The middle adult needs to make sense of his in-between place in life. He needs to learn to become young/old in a different way than in early adulthood.

2. Destruction/Creation. The middle-aged man is more aware of the coming death and destruction of himself than ever before. He is also aware of hurts that he has absorbed and hurts he has inflicted. Yet he has a strong desire to become more creative and to contribute more fully to coming generations as well.

3. Masculine/Feminine. The male needs to deal with masculine/feminine polarities in many areas, such as body prowess, achievement and ambition, power and weakness, thinking and feeling. The basic assumption is that men are logical, reasonable, analytical, intellectual, and interested in how things work. Women, in turn, are assumed to be more emotional, intuitive, dependent, and more aware of their feelings. As one achieves mid-life individuation, one needs to search for a more appropriate combination of these "masculine" and "feminine" qualities in oneself.

4. Attachment/Separateness. To be attached is to be engaged, involved, rooted, and participating. To be separate is to be primarily involved in one's own inner world of imagination, fantasy, play,

contemplation, and reflection. A person may have had times in life when one overemphasized one of these polarities at the expense of the other. A major task of middle adulthood is to find a more appropriate balance between the needs of the self and the needs of society.

In summary, then, these are life tasks of middle-age men: building and modifying the life structure; working on single components of the life structure; achieving identity or individuation.

It is at this point that Levinson's investigation ends. Though he speculates about later adult years, we will not summarize that preliminary thinking at this point.

Roger Gould, Transformations

Out of his work of supervising psychiatric doctoral students at UCLA, Roger Gould began to be aware that certain needs and problems were "age related." That is, in time, he found he could predict what problems a patient would be facing at each life stage.

Following the preliminary noting of the concerns of patients of various ages, Gould did research with more than five hundred people who were not psychiatric patients. He discovered that patients and nonpatients of the same age shared the same broad concerns about living. Out of this study, he gained a general outline of the changing patterns of self-awareness that occur in men and women between the ages of sixteen and fifty.

Gould writes:

> I concluded . . . that *adulthood is not a plateau;* rather, it is a dynamic and changing time for all of us. As we grow and change, we take steps *away* from childhood and *toward* adulthood—steps such as marriage, work, consciously developing a talent or buying a home. With each step, the unfinished business of childhood intrudes, disturbing our emotions and requiring psychological work. With this in mind, adults may now view their disturbed feelings at particular periods as a possible sign of progress, as part of their attempted movement toward a fuller adult life.[14]

Gould sees the adult as progressively correcting the misconceptions of what he calls *"childhood consciousness."* He points out that while most adults wistfully recall childhood as carefree and exuberant, they largely forget the other side of childhood. In childhood there is also "the powerful larger-than-life anger and hurt all children experience as they cope with the world."[15] Gould calls this potentially uncontrollable destructiveness by the term "demonic anger." He contends this demon, anger, is the key ingredient of childhood consciousness that must be mastered. Gould contends, *"Even if our parents loved us with perfect empathy and understanding, we all feel let down in some way and bear the scars to prove it."*[16]

What triggers the demonic anger in adult life? Gould contends that both in children and in adults this anger is aroused each time we encounter a separation situation. For the child, it is a physical separation. For the adult, it is a love separation; that is, we feel misunderstood, mislabeled, or slighted.

As adults, though we are sensitive to any signs of loss of love, we usually don't respond with the primitive demonic anger. We've probably gained adult perspectives and adult methods of coping. However, occasionally we lose perspective; we blow up. But then in these crises (which may have to do with love or authority), this childlike view of reality can revisit the adult with a tremendous power. "We are then faced with two realities: *current reality*—the reality of adult consciousness, the way we actually experience events and each other now; and *demonic reality*—the childhood consciousness reality, the intrusion into adult life of painful childhood states."[17]

This leads Gould to the basic principle of his book: *"By striving for a fuller, more independent adult consciousness, we trigger the angry demons of childhood consciousness. Growing and reformulating our self-definition becomes a dangerous act. It is the act of transformation."*[18]

In Gould's understanding then, adult consciousness develops between the ages of sixteen and fifty by mastering our childhood fears and by learning to control and modulate our childhood anger which is released by change. In our development as adults we encounter layer after layer of buried childhood pains. Our adult consciousness evolves through a series of confrontations with our own childhood past. As adults we become progressively more able to confront and master the demonic realities and rework the irrationalities of childhood.

Gould suggests that the childhood consciousness is based on four major false assumptions that children believe. They are the following:

1. We'll always live with our parents and be their child.
2. They'll always be there to help when we can't do something on our own.
3. Their simplified version of our complicated inner reality is correct, as

when they turn the light on in our bedroom to prove there are no ghosts.
4. There is no real death or evil in the world. [19]

Although by the end of high school we know these assumptions are factually incorrect, they retain hidden control of our adult experience until we are able to detect them as emotional as well as intellectual fantasies.

Gould's understanding of adult life stages is that one of these assumptions is challenged in each stage of life.

The first assumption, "I'll always belong to my parents," comes under question during the years eighteen to twenty-two when the individual lives away from home and takes on beliefs or actions that seem appropriate but don't fit parental life-style and beliefs.

The second assumption, "They (my parents) will always be there to help me," is most powerfully challenged in our twenties when we are setting up an independent life and making important decisions that no one else can make for us—career, marriage, pregnancy, etc. We substitute our own proven competence for this false assumption.

The third assumption, "Life is simple and controllable," is challenged in our late twenties and early thirties. At that time in life, "the simple rules and supposed-to-be's about life prove ineffectual in the complicated real world." The discovery of the amazing complexity of both inner and outer worlds, the acceptance of that complexity and the choice of life-style based on conscious choice in that complexity requires the shedding of the third childhood assumption.

The fourth assumption, "There is no evil or death in the world," is challenged in the late thirties through forties. Time pressures mount; parents and other persons important to a person die; children go out of one's life. The illusion must be destroyed if one is to face finitude and mortality with integrity and creativity.[20]

This, then, is Gould's concept of life stages, that progressively throughout our lives, we come to grips with the "demons" of "childhood consciousness." To the extent people succeed in shedding the assumptions of childhood, they are transformed into growing, becoming adults.

Gail Sheehy, Passages

My little survey of some recent explorations of middle age would be most incomplete if I neglected mentioning the best-selling

Passages. [21] Gail Sheehy is a journalist who was initially stimulated to explore this field by her own mid-life crisis. She, also, turned to Erikson, Levinson, and Gould, among others, in her search. Their earlier research, combined with her own intensive interviews of 115 men and women, aided her in her sensitive treatment of life stages. She contends that no life structure lasts more than seven years. One is then confronted with a crisis demanding adjustment and change. However, since most people misunderstand the term "crisis," which is a turning point, she has used a less threatening term to describe these critical transitions between life stages. Instead, she calls them "passages," and, thus, the title of her book.

Since she builds on the findings of the writers we have already discussed, and since we will be benefiting from her insights in the following chapters, we will not outline her work here. It has marked similarities to those already cited. Anyone desiring a more detailed look at life stages should certainly consult this accessible, readable book.

Iris Sangiuliano, In Her Time

Earlier I noted some discontent about "Life Stage" theories of adult development. I expressed some personal resistance where one theory did not seem to fit me. Some have felt that a more holistic concept of adult growth is needed. Others have suggested that perhaps life stages are a contrived device which contributes to a "self-fulfilling prophecy." That is to say, "Since the scientists say I'm supposed to go through these stages, I'll go through them!"

Iris Sangiuliano, who intensively interviewed a small group of middle-class women who were or had been married, is a critic of the Life Stage theory, also. She says that, like most theoretical constructions, the Life Stage theory has its shortcomings. One of them is in regard to predictability. She asks, "Has anyone known a woman's life that was predictable?" She points to the myriad of influences that shape any individual life—social climate and expectations, personal psychological response; she finds no predictable pattern.

But she finds these theories lacking on the question of unpredictability as well. She finds that unexpected critical events change the focus and direction of women's lives. She writes, "... I was struck by the fact that women's lives unfold, not in a rigid, predictable progression of conflicts, identity, mastery, and autonomy, but rather in great surges of billowing change." [22]

Sangiuliano notes a slower, more arduous development of identity for women than for men. Men are groomed *to do,* while women are taught *to be.* Boys have to earn their masculine identity while feminine identity is ascribed to girls' puberty. The result is "a significant delay in the girl's search for identity. . . ." [23]

This continues into adult life. For the most part, she feels that women are "late bloomers" who postpone themselves. She sees women living a life derived from the male experience. This is true whether the woman is in the home or the corporate office.

The women she studied expected to be married and succeeded in accomplishing that. They first thought in terms of "we." And then, at some time, they discovered the "I," within the "we" or outside the "we."

How does this emergence of the "I" occur? She quotes sculptor Louise Nevelson, "Most of us have to be transplanted, like a tree, before we blossom." [24] Disruption, contradiction, paradox—these can be the occasions for growth and self-discovery.

She cites approvingly the theory of Klaus Reigel. Reigel notes that adult development encompasses simultaneous movement along four dimensions: "(1) inner-biological, (2) individual-psychological, (3) cultural-sociological, and (4) outer-physical." As progression within or between those dimensions occurs, crises, which can be growth producing, may ensue.

Sangiuliano speaks of such crises as the following:

—"a life-threatening illness (inner-biological)";

—"the contradiction of merger and distancing necessary for development"; for example, the discovery that a wife can no longer absorb herself in her husband's identity (individual-psychological);

—discovering that one is out of step with social environs, such as the woman whose husband had joined the back-to-earth movement and had bought a farm, and then she discovered she had no interest in baking bread or making sausages (cultural-sociological);

—wars, famines, floods, pestilence (outer-physical). [25]

Sangiuliano points out many events which can be these pivotal events in a woman's life, such as the beginning of menstruation or its cessation, marriage, motherhood, divorce, illness, and death. But what makes the event *critical* is the element of the *unexpected.*

Anticipated or familiar catastrophes seem to be discounted.

> Instead, it is the disruption of deeply ingrained attitudes and expectations about sex, marriage, motherhood, and work that causes major upheavals and transitions. In short, unless we disrupt the old and the familiar and suffer the disenchantments, there's no room for the new.[26]

I feel that Sangiuliano has perhaps overcriticized the Life Stage view of adult development. This view was good news to me, for it heralded dynamic growth and change for adults throughout a lifetime. Furthermore, I never viewed stages as overly binding or rigid. Rather, they seemed to me to be like the structure of a short story or a symphony. The possibilities of variations within were endless.

Nevertheless, she offers a most valuable differing viewpoint. An insightful view of women's development by a woman psychotherapist, Sangiuliano's book highlights the importance of the unpredictable shattering event precipitating growth and identity *at any point* (but usually after the weakening of the "we" mentality) in a woman's life.

What, Then, Is Middle Age?

What is middle age? It is, first of all, a period of life. What period? Students of this life stage don't agree. Some say it may be thirty years long, from age thirty to age sixty. More likely, the period of life from the late thirties to the mid-fifties is the duration of time that properly belongs in this designation.

It is, second, a state of mind. One's consciousness and view of life change as one senses the passing of time. For many of us there is a new "this is it" feeling about the decisions at mid-life. There are issues of a new depth to be faced.

It is, third, a challenge to face the shadows and dark places in one's life. Mortality, failure of achievement and relationship, unfulfilled dreams—all become distressingly apparent and important during this period of life.

But it is, fourth, an opportunity to explore all of the possibilities of growth, creativity, and becoming for the rest of one's life.

Fifth, it is the opportunity to do mid-course correction in the voyage through life so that one will reach the destination one truly desires and not let one's future be something that just happens.

Sixth, middle age is a time of great responsibility. Lest the preceding descriptions make this time of life sound like a quiet, introspective search, it should be added that persons in this life stage run the nation's businesses, industries, institutions, and governments; manage its finances; and give significant community service. They also guide and raise teenage and young adult children, provide for their education, and guide them into this same world. For many, middle age is self-examination and decision making on the run! Finally, mid-life is a time to claim Eda LeShan's upbeat promise, "I believe deeply that for those of us who are middle-aged, the most profound growing still lies ahead of us."[27]

Faith and Mid-Life Issues

We who share the Christian faith need to discover the profound faith implications of what these life stage researchers have been saying to us. Each of these authors speaks of the management of a limited, finite life. Each speaks of growth and development that are to take place in the depths of a person's being. There are direct connections between these concepts of life management and inner growth and the teachings of the Christian faith. Indeed, our faith illumines these processes and gives them added dimensions.

Take, for example, the title and theme of Gail Sheehy's book, *Passages.* One perceptive reviewer made this comparison:

> [Sheehy] has . . . produced today's secular version of that grand old life map provided for our ancestors by John Bunyan in *Pilgrim's Progress,* though the "sins" of her book are of omission rather than of commission, and the final goal, Bunyan's heaven, is Sheehy's liberation from self. The two goals are not dissimilar.[28]

As Sheehy describes for me a pilgrimage through life, I find myself recalling a similar pilgrimage through life:

> By faith Abraham obeyed when he was called to go out to a place which he was to receive as an inheritance; and he went out, not knowing where he was to go. By faith he sojourned in a land of promise, as in a foreign land, living in tents with Isaac and Jacob, heirs with him of the same promise. For he looked forward to the city which has foundations, whose builder and maker is God (Hebrews 11:8-10).

I find Sheehy right-on in the pilgrimage she describes. My faith perspective tells me I conduct my pilgrimage before God, with God, to God. Thus, there are other elements of the pilgrimage that must be explored.

Further, when Levinson speaks to me of "the seasons of a man's life," I find myself thinking of Psalm 90, that great expression of God's eternity and human finitude,

> The years of our life are threescore and ten,
>   or even by reason of strength fourscore;
> yet their span is but toil and trouble;
>   they are soon gone and we fly away.
> . . . . .
> So teach us to number our days
>   that we may get a heart of wisdom.
> —Psalm 90:10, 12

The seasons of a person's life are short. There is much to be done. However, proper management of life and hope about its possibilities are offered to the person of faith.

Finally, when Gould speaks of transformations which come when we overcome the "demons" of childhood consciousness, he is speaking in theological terms. I suspect that Gould is consciously giving psychological interpretation to these belief terms. But we who read Gould's works with eyes of faith can turn the tables as well. For we live in fellowship with the one who casts out demons. Indeed, he once cast out a demon in answer to a desperate cry, "I believe; help my unbelief!" (Mark 9:24).

And when I hear Sangiuliano speaking of a second birth, I find myself asking again with Nicodemus, "How can a man be born when he is old? Can he enter a second time into his mother's womb and be born?" (John 3:4). I am answered by the One who makes transformation-rebirth a constant possibility.

As I told you, I suffered considerable pain and depression when I reached my mid-life crisis. Therefore, I am deeply grateful to these authors for the analysis and hope they offer me. They have helped me understand myself better. When I am in touch with my Source, I believe their hope about transformation and growth, only more so!

3

CONFRONTED WITH THE ARITHMETIC OF LIFE

Facing My Own Finitude

"Without warning, in the middle of my thirties, I had a breakdown of nerve."[1] So Gail Sheehy starts her remarkable book, *Passages*. She tells of an experience she had when she was working as a journalist in northern Ireland. While she was interviewing a young boy after they had triumphantly participated in a civil rights march, suddenly live ammunition was in the air. She saw his face hit and mangled by a bullet. Up to that moment, she says, she had thought that everything could be mended.

After the shocking attack was over, she found herself in a city that for a time was closed to all travel. She had nothing to do but wait. She attempted to pray. Then she tried to call the man she loved. But nothing brought any comfort. In the dread waiting a powerful idea took hold of her, *"No one is with me. No one can keep me safe. There is no one who won't ever leave me alone."* She says, "I had a headache for a year."[2]

Upon her return from Ireland, this confrontation with her own mortality occasioned more brooding over the shortness of her life span. She reflected on the many things she had hoped to accomplish in it. She relates, "To be confronted for the first time with the arithmetic of life was, quite simply, terrifying."[3]

For Sheehy, this anxiety took many forms—fear of flying, inability to write, and physical ailments, among others. The ways to deal with this anxiety are equally diverse. She suggests three that are frequently tried. First, "turn on the lights. It always made the spooks go away in childhood." Look for a clear and simple medical explanation. Second, call for help. Find the strong one who can interrupt the fear and make it disappear. Third, try to ignore it by keeping busy; fill your life with so many activities that you can mask free-floating anxiety.[4] Unfortunately, none of these techniques work. One will need to find new ways to deal with this central issue of mid-life.

> Each of us stumbles upon the major issue of midlife somewhere in the decade between 35 and 45. Though this can also be an ordinary passage with no outer event to mark it, eventually we all confront the reality of our own death. And somehow, we must learn to live with it. The first time that this message comes through is probably the worst.[5]

Many students of mid-life agree that this is indeed the central task of mid-life, coming to terms with one's own finitude and death.

I hesitate to call this a universal mid-life experience. Some of my women friends do not experience this encounter with finitude as part of their mid-life transition at all. These are persons who have been primarily occupied with being homemaker and mother. In mid-life, these demands on their time and energies decrease. They find themselves facing a much different and, as yet undefined, future. Life, not death, stands before them.

I'm not quite sure what to make of a woman's experience. Perhaps she has already faced her finitude when undergoing anesthesia and childbirth. Perhaps some of her immortality needs have been met through bearing and nurturing children who now have grown and live out her influence. Or perhaps the death-finitude issue still awaits her further down the road of life after she has resolved the immediate vocational issues.

It may be that men experience the biggest shock when they become aware of death because finally they encounter something (mortality) they cannot control. Perhaps women in our culture are more accustomed to "giving themselves over" to some other power and, thus, recognize their dependence, frailty, and mortality. Possibly a woman's body cycle keeps her more in touch with her mortal body, with menopause serving as a consciousness-raising event that says in effect to the woman, "You are not going any further into life now, you

are going toward the end, to the absolute determinism of death."[6]
At any rate, each person comes to a time she or he must come to grips with her or his own finitude. Some time in mid-life is usually the time when that subject simply cannot be avoided any longer.

However, if facing one's death and finitude is a central mid-life task, it is also the most difficult. Some would say that handling this subject with any sense of peace is nearly impossible.

Ernest Becker, in his Pulitzer Prize winning work, *The Denial of Death*, has explored how humanity denies, ignores, and represses the subject of death. He argues that our horror of death is a mainspring of our drive for success, heroics, and business. "The idea of death, the fear of it, haunts the human animal like nothing else; it is a mainspring of human activity—activity designed largely to avoid the fatality of death, to overcome it by denying in some way that it is the final destiny for man."[7]

Becker writes:

Man has a symbolic identity that brings him sharply out of nature. He is . . . a creature with a name, a life history. . . . a mind that soars out to speculate about atoms and infinity. . . . This immense expansion . . . this self-consciousness gives to man literally the status of a small god in nature, as the Renaissance thinkers knew.

Yet, at the same time, as the Eastern sages also knew, man is a worm and food for worms. This is the paradox: he is out of nature and hopelessly in it; he is dual, up in the stars and yet housed in a heart-pumping, breath-gasping body. . . . His body is a material fleshy casing that is alien to him in many ways—the strangest and most repugnant way being that it aches and bleeds and will decay and die. Man is literally split in two: he has an awareness of his own splendid uniqueness in that he sticks out of nature and a towering majesty, and yet he goes back into the ground a few feet in order blindly and dumbly to rot and disappear forever. It is a terrifying dilemma to be in and to have to live with.[8]

When it is so starkly put, this finitude dilemma seems to be too much for the human personality to handle. Therefore, what does one do?

He literally drives himself into a blind obliviousness with social games, psychological tricks, personal preoccupations so far removed from the reality of his situation that they are forms of madness—agreed madness, shared madness, disguised and dignified madness, but madness is all the same.[9]

I have no doubt that Becker describes a nearly universal response to the subject of death. But must it be so? Really, is it such a curse to be granted god-like creativity and yet be sentenced to limited life on this planet? Are our accomplishments then wasted? Is finitude insulting to us as we walk closer to the termination of our lives? Should we not consider the possibility that, though our bodies are indeed destroyed in death, there may be some hope of immortality for us? Should we not consult with those who have lived closer to dying? Should we ask them if that blanket repression of death of which Becker speaks is necessary?

If we discover that we are not in control and that heroism and bravado fail us, what resources are available to help us face our finitude?

At this point we can benefit from the counsel of Elisabeth Kübler-Ross, that person who discovered what the dying have to teach us. Dr. Kübler-Ross has suggested how helpful it would be if more of us would talk about death and dying as an intrinsic part of life, just as we freely discuss birth. If we did this, it would be a much more simple task to help a patient deal with a terminal illness, she says.[10] She prefers discussing death and dying with patients long before it actually happens, if the patient indicates a readiness for that. In her opinion, "a healthier, stronger individual can deal with it better and be less frightened by oncoming death when it is still 'miles away' than when it is 'right in front of the door.'"[11]

Well, we are presumably "miles away" from our deaths, but they are coming. Living is a terminal situation. Quite possibly, during teenage and early adult years, the major developmental tasks (identity, intimacy, etc.,) are so heavy that persons *have* to repress the dilemma of death in order to get the other tasks worked out. But now in the middle years the time in life has come really to "look" at death, to "unrepress" that dreaded and frightening subject.

But how does one do that? For when one speaks of death, one describes (in Tillich's terms) an "existential anxiety," not a "neurotic anxiety." This death anxiety cannot be removed by pills or positive thinking or psychoanalysis.

I was one whose death anxiety bubbled around in my consciousness for several months, causing acute distress. I would not have been helped if someone had put a hand on my shoulder and said, "Straighten out and accept your creaturely existence." My creaturely existence was the problem!

Still, there are steps which can be taken to deal with death anxiety. Consider the terms "unrepress," "deal with," "work out" (that phrase brings to mind the not unrelated Bible verses, ". . . work out your own salvation with fear and trembling; for God is at work in you . . ." [Philippians 2:12-13]), or "grief work." These terms imply one needs not remain immobilized by panic. A person can face an issue, absorb its truth down into the depth of one's being, and sense community with other persons and their support in this dilemma. These are ultimately steps of faith in our Source.

To help in this process, I am going to share some material with you. The purpose of this is to raise consciousness and help each person examine attitudes. One may not feel as free to choose as the material implies. Still, we live with these issues. Each person may be granted the courage to live more fully and consciously in the light of his or her ultimate death.

What are some of the existing attitudes toward finitude?

J. William Worden and William Proctor help us at this point with their concept of "Personal Death Awareness." As you would expect, personal death awareness is sensitivity to your own limited life span and the fact that some day you will die. They give the following three examples of levels of death awareness that were discerned in patients:

1. *Very Low Personal Death Awareness.* Sam was a fifty-five-year-old man who had not been able to tolerate funerals, wakes, or hospitals. Admitted to the hospital and diagnosed as having advanced terminal stomach cancer, he refused to accept the diagnosis. Though he lost weight and strength, he insisted he would be back to work soon. He refused to affirm his religious beliefs or accept the ministries of his priest. He failed to prepare his wife for living alone. He did not discuss plans for funeral and burial. He died without a will. Worden and Proctor conclude, "Sam's life-style—his previous stress on the importance of marital love, efficiency in his daily affairs, and a firm religious faith—was abandoned in his death style of denial." [12]

2. *Very High Personal Death Awareness.* Lisa, a school teacher twenty-seven years of age, was frequently preoccupied with her own death. Bad dreams of death and anxieties caused her occasionally to miss work. She refused to believe that a previous case of hepatitus (a fairly common liver disease) was really cured, and she returned to the

hospital frequently for additional liver tests. She would refuse to believe the negative results and thought she was going to die of this illness in the near future. Friends were turned off by her fear of a shortened life. She found herself angry and alone.

Lisa turned to psychotherapy and discovered the reason for her preoccupation with death. Her father had died when she was thirteen. He had been an alcoholic and had been estranged from the family. When he died, the family expressed their anger at him by a quick, private funeral, cremation, and spreading of the ashes. Though Lisa, the youngest child, objected, the family proceeded with these plans. She felt angry and hopelessly frustrated.

Therapy helped her get in touch with her obsessive fear of death. Her fear was that she would end up like her father, dead with no one caring. By discovering the roots of her fear, she brought her Personal Death Awareness to a more manageable level.

3. *Moderate Personal Death Awareness.* Jack was a thirty-year-old, husband and father of six, with a terminal kidney ailment. Every medical treatment was tried, including two kidney transplants, but neither worked because of his body's susceptibility to infection. Though he hoped for another donor, he finally realized the donor would never arrive. His first reaction was irritability. Then, this phase passed, and he assumed a realistic attitude toward his limited life span. He began to discuss his situation frankly with his wife. They found themselves able to cry together. This in turn opened up communication so that they could make plans for the present and the future. They discussed every relevant topic—mortgage payments, driver's lessons for his non-driving wife, domestic chores, and financial responsibilities. He told her he wanted a simple burial to save money for the children's education. He expressed the desire that his body be used to serve; he wanted his eyes donated to people who needed them. They expressed their love for each other and communicated the coming death with the children. When he died, the children decided to assume responsibility for their father's cemetery plot, taking turns.[13]

Worden and Proctor, in reflecting on such experiences, point out that although you cannot choose whether to die or not, you can exercise quite a few other options.

You can choose:
• How you view death.

- To recognize that you have a limited life span and begin to order your life on that basis.
- To let an understanding of your death intensify and improve your present relationships.
- What to do with your body when you're finished with it.
- How you want to be remembered by friends and family.
- Where you would like to die.
- To fear death less.
- To learn to talk more comfortably about death.
- To get the psychological upper hand over a terminal illness.
- Not to continue living on artificial, extraordinary support systems.
- Whether or not to end your own life.
- Whether or not to draw up a will.
- Whether or not to carry life insurance.
- To develop resources for confronting death.[14]

How does one move from the denial of death to the personal death awareness of which Worden and Proctor speak? Again we may be guided by the findings of Dr. Kübler-Ross. She has discovered that terminally ill persons go through five stages of dying. While not all persons experience all the stages, still her discovery provides a valuable map. Further, a person does not necessarily leave one stage to go on to the others. A person may vacillate between the stages at times, but the map is still insightful.

I am going to explore Kübler-Ross's stages of dying and some other studies of terminally ill patients. Then I intend to "reason backward" from these patients to the mortality dilemma of middle adults. I am going to do this for two reasons: *(a)* I share Kübler-Ross's conviction that the dying have much to teach us; *(b)* this seems to be the only material available on this subject. Many volumes on middle-age give a brief nod to the subject of death and quickly pass on to more pleasant topics.

Since the issue is so basic, I will take the available material and try to glean the significant discoveries for us mid-lifers. These, then, are the five stages of dying as Kübler-Ross conceives them:[15]

1. Denial. "No, not me." As a first response to news of coming death, denial is important and a very common step, as it helps cushion the impact of the dread news.

2. Rage and anger. "Why me?" The patient is likely to be most resentful that he or she will die while others remain healthy and alive. The anger may be general and vague, or it may be directed at God, physician and hospital staff, the family, or all of them.

3. Bargaining. "Yes, me, but. . . ." The patient begins to accept the fact of one's death but bargains for more time.

4. Depression. "Yes, me." Here there are two types of depression: reactive and preparatory. The person experiencing reactive depression mourns past losses, tasks not accomplished, wrongs committed. Then one moves on to a state of preparatory grief as one prepares for the loss of all living experience, all present objects of love. During this stage a person may withdraw from persons around one, having finished one's business with them. However, those standing by should not abandon the patient; they should be understanding if the patient needs their presence less.

5. Acceptance. "My time is very close, and it's all right." [16]

In chart form, the road map of the stages of dying looks like this. [17]

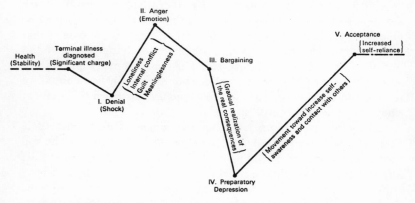

Elisabeth Kübler-Ross, *Death, the Final Stage of Growth* (Englewood Cliffs, N.J.: Prentice-Hall, Inc. 1975).

As I earlier implied, these stages inform not only the course of the terminal patient. They also provide some insight for the mid-life person as he or she makes the pilgrimage through life to death. Note that these five stages start with denial, that very term Becker said was the basic attitude toward death in our society. He is right. Society denies that death exists. So do funeral homes, hospitals, and most persons in their childhood, youth, and young adult years. But then comes the mid-life crisis. Changing bodies, death of parents, and other events make it less possible to deny death as a personal future event.

Because one's death seems at a reasonably safe distance, I suspect that most mid-lifers combine stages 2, 3, and 4; that is, rage and anger, bargaining, and depression. What they do experience is limited time, frustration of dreams, and increasing bodily reminders of finitude. They discover that one life will not be long enough to do all the things they had hoped to do.

The mid-lifer comes to the conclusion, not that "time is up," but rather that "time is short." Out of this awareness can come the most wise stewardship of time. It might be well to imagine oneself terminally ill and ask, "If I were dying, what would be the relationships I would most savor, the tasks in which I would take most pride, the beliefs and causes that I would want to perpetuate?" Then one can resolve to come to death with as little depression over unlived life as possible.

Sometime, usually near the end of middle-age years, a person can move onto the stage of acceptance. "I want to live as long and as well as possible, but somehow, death is going to be all right." When, during mid-life, a person has gone beyond the all-common death denial of our society and achieved a measure of acceptance, then one can be assured that he or she will much more calmly face the final act of dying.

There is one more matter that is important in helping one come to acceptance of death. One needs to know that it mattered that she or he lived. If one cannot be around consciously participating in the events in future generations, can he or she at least know that in some way he or she endures?

Robert Lifton and Eric Olson address this question with their concept of "symbolic immortality." They suggest that one experiences a sense of immortality in five "modes" or categories. (These modes may be more meaningful in some cultures than in others.)

The *first* mode is *"biological* immortality" which means that one lives on through sons and daughters and their sons and daughters.

Second is the mode of *"works"* or the *"creative"* mode. "One may feel a sense of immortality . . . through teaching, art-making, repairing, construction, writing, healing, inventing, or through lasting influences of any kind on other human beings—influences that one feels can enter into a general human flow beyond the self."[18]

Third, the *"theological* mode of immortality" is that set of beliefs that affirms the person's place in the eternal plans of God.

The *"fourth* mode is immortality achieved through *continuity with nature.*" "You are dust, and to dust you shall return" (Genesis 3:19) is not only an Old Testament warning against pride, but it is also the affirmation of affinity with nature that endures beyond the person, but of which the person is a part. Whatever happens to human beings, trees, mountains, rivers, and seas endures. We sense this and return to nature for spiritual refreshment and revitalization.

A *fifth* mode of immortality is *"experiential transcendence"*; that is, going beyond the limits and confines of ordinary daily life in some experience of ecstasy. This might be found in a religious encounter, but it may also be found in "music, dance, battle, athletics, mechanical flight, contemplation of the past, artistic or intellectual creation, sexual love, childbirth, comradeship, and the feeling of working together with others in common cause." [19]

Therefore, say Lifton and Olson, five modes are available to us to participate in that which endures. Within these modes we are granted symbolic immortality.

We may reach a state when we are assured that we partake in that which will endure. We begin to understand that death is part of living. We progress on to a preliminary participation in the last stage of attitudes toward dying—acceptance. Our search at mid-life is ultimately a spiritual one.

Then a serendipity occurs. Acceptance of death makes us more truly alive, more open to growth and becoming. Aware that we don't have endless time in this universe, we begin to concentrate on that which really matters. Again, we can see this most clearly among the terminally ill, but it is true for all of us. Murray L. Trelease, in recalling his experience among Indians in Seattle, writes:

> I remember a nineteen year old boy dying of leukemia who in two weeks' time grew from a rather irresponsible brat to a loving, understanding counselor who led his family through the shattering experience of his dying. When he first learned he was dying he could think of nothing but rejection and resentment. But a short time later he discovered that he had a long agenda of things he wanted to know and understand. There were people to see, old sores to heal, his family to help and comfort; he was still thinking of more things to accomplish when he died suddenly. . . . the sentence of death . . . may mark the beginning of the greatest growth of a lifetime in understanding, love, and faith.[20]

May it be so with persons at mid-life. May acceptance of our finitude propel us into the most lovely type of becoming.

Faith and Finitude

What is the connection between the Christian faith and our finitude? There are several interrelationships that readily come to mind.

First, there is the discovery of Dr. Kübler-Ross that while nominal or external religion is no help at all to dying people (and is sometimes a hindrance), "intensely religious people accept death more easily than others . . . if they are authentic and have internalized their faith. The significant variable is . . . how truly and genuinely you believe. Truly religious people with a deep abiding relationship with God have found it much easier to face death with equanimity."[21]

Second, however, there is a caution we must consider. I fear that often people of faith have participated in that death denial that Becker found so pervasive in our culture. What I mean is that we speak so glibly of heaven, life after death, resurrection, etc., that we ignore and deny the reality of death. Whatever the Christian faith promises, it does not promise that Christians escape dying. An individual still must come to grips with his or her own dying and must die by oneself, the alone with the alone. When someone you care about dies before you, the Christian is not spared any of the loneliness, agony, or grief work that accompanies such a loss.

Therefore, the Christian must be careful not to overclaim or underclaim what the Christian faith may provide in the face of death. One overclaims when one insists that our faith makes dying something one does easily, with eager anticipation. (Frankly, many pop Christian songs about dying and heaven fall into just this error.) But one should not underclaim what the Christian faith offers in this regard either, for both the New Testament and contemporary believers show us that our faith helps one face death openly with trust and hope. In short, what faith offers is death transformation, not death denial. But I will discuss this further in a moment.

Third, Jesus, the central figure of our faith, lived among us, suffered, and died. As I read those detailed accounts in the Gospels, I detect that he went through stages of dying similar to those Kübler-Ross described. For example, is there not possible bargaining, anger, and depression in our Master's words, "My Father, if it be possible, let this cup pass from me" (Matthew 26:39); "My God, my God, why hast thou forsaken me?" (Matthew 27:46); "It is finished" (John 19:30)? Then in his final moments, is there not the mood of acceptance, "Father, into thy hands I commit my spirit!" (Luke 23:46)? Further, Hebrews 5:7 reminds us, "In the days of his flesh, Jesus offered up prayers and supplications, with loud cries and tears, to him who was able to save him from death. . . ."

My personal belief is strengthened by this discovery. I discover my Master entered so fully into my humanity that he died with similar emotions and personal processes that I must face. He models for me how to die and offers me knowledgeable companionship as I face the fact of my own death.

By his entering into the process of dying with and for us, he conquered sin and death. The victory established through his death means that death is transformed. We die from a different perspective than we would without him (Hebrews 2:14-15; 1 Corinthians 15:57).

Fourth, as I seek my "symbolic immortality" of which Lifton speaks, I find the consolations of the Christian faith at every point:

Biological Immortality—In the very process of begetting children I have been drawn up into partnership with God and have become creator with God. The Old Testament affirms that children are a means to immortality in that one's influence and name are perpetuated.

"Works" or "Creative" Immortality—Recall the final verse of Psalm 90, that great poem on God's eternity and our mortality.

Let the favor of the Lord our God be upon us
    and establish thou the work of our hands upon us,
yea, the work of our hands establish thou it.

Psalm 90:17

The psalmist trustfully asks God to take the things he had done, accept them, and "establish them," make them endure.

Immortality Through Continuity with Nature. Our faith affirms this channel as well.

I will lift up my eyes to the hills.
From whence does my help come?
My help comes from the LORD,
Who made heaven and earth.

—Psalm 121:1

Immortality Through "Experiential Transcendence," that is, experiences of ecstasy wherever they occur. The Bible tells us that our experiences of fellowship with God, those moments of ecstasy, are the preview sample of the glory we will share. Jesus tells us, "And this is eternal life, that they know thee, the only true God, and Jesus Christ whom thou hast sent" (John 17:3). Since we affirm a God who created all, we have no problem accepting the idea that any moment of ecstasy in music, art, contemplation, comradeship, etc., is indeed a gift of God symbolizing that which meaningfully endures.

While these four of Lifton's and Olson's "modes" of "symbolic immortality" are not ignored in biblical faith, we must pause for a caution. None of these four is distinctively Christian. Furthermore, neither "biological immortality" nor "works or creative immortality" is available to all. Further still, dependence on these four modes would be idolatry, as they are modes which "trust" in blood lines (children), creative works (works of righteousness), nature worship, or the self. These modes do have important meanings, but these meanings must be peripheral for the Christian, never central. This brings us to the central mode for the Christian.

Theological Immortality. As I implied earlier, our Christian faith offers a theological view of death transformed, not death denied. Jesus' resurrection was a new and powerful divine event in the world. Though Jesus died with all the dread you or I experience, God acted upon that death to confirm Jesus' costly sacrifice, to awaken us to Jesus' continued power and influence in the world, and to assure us that "whether we live or whether we die, we are the Lord's" (Romans 14:8).

When we discover how gently our Christian faith leads us into the acceptance of death with trust and hope, we are ready to hear Dr. Kübler-Ross's word that comes at the conclusion of much massive firsthand study and conversations with dying persons. She writes the following:

"Death is the final stage of growth in this life. There is not total death. Only the body dies. The self or spirit, or whatever you may wish to label it, is eternal." [22]

We are ready, too, for her counsel as to how to live in the light of this knowledge.

In order to be at peace, it is necessary to feel a sense of history—that you are both part of what has come before and part of what is yet to come. Being thus surrounded, you are not alone; and the sense of urgency that pervades the present is put in perspective: Do not frivolously use the time- that is yours to spend. Cherish it, that each day may bring new growth, insight, and awareness. Use this growth not selfishly, but rather in service of what may be, in the future tide of time. Never allow a day to pass that did not add to what was understood before. Let each day be a stone in the path of growth. Do not rest until what was intended has been done. But remember—go as slowly as is necessary in order to sustain a steady pace; do not expend energy in waste. Finally, do not allow the illusory urgencies of the immediate to distract you from your vision of the eternal. . . .[23]

4

DO YOU WANT TO BE WHOLE?

Health Management for the Middle Adult

"Is this you? You put antifreeze in your car *after* the temperature goes below zero. You buy tires *after* the first heavy snow?"[1] If so, you're probably also the type who thinks that health catastrophes happen to someone else and not to you.

But now, you're middle-aged, and that sort of wishful thinking has to go. The truth of your own mortality has dawned upon you with force. With that realization comes an eagerness to live as well and as long as possible. After all, you have a great deal to do in this limited-span lifetime. In regard to your health, it is time to stop drifting and start navigating. Choose to be more intentional and more wise about your body than you have ever been before.

Dr. William Barclay, chairman of the American Medical Association's Committee on Hypertension, points out that health maintenance generally has a very low priority in this country. Usually one gets concerned only after becoming sick. He concludes, "If we could change people's habits, we'd have a tremendous impact."[2]

John McCann, medical director of the Life Extension Institute, points out:

> . . . without question, the greatest untapped resource of health care in this country is the individual himself; the potential capability that is available

in each of us to properly control and alter our living habits. The evidence is in: Whether you live or die is often squarely in your own hands.[3]

Therefore, let us explore what each of us can do in the pursuit of health.

Health and Our Cardiovascular System

A recent copy of *Bostonia* magazine[4] provided a lay guide to cardiovascular disease to help all of us be more informed, wise, and responsible about our health. I shall briefly summarize their observations and recommendations.

The authors point out that 50 percent of all deaths in the United States are a result of cardiovascular disease. They suggest also that preventing heart attack and stroke, while it takes work, may add twenty or more years to a person's life. If one considers those twenty years worth saving, then one needs to choose to pay intentional attention to one's health and to take action to maintain one's health.

They point out that atherosclerosis (a disease which occurs when "the inner layer of the artery wall is thickened by cellular material and deposits of several substances, particularly fats") is the major cause of death in the United States. Most of us know this disease better by the names of its two major complications: heart attack and stroke.

"The cardiovascular system consists of the heart and all the blood vessels in the body." When the inner layers of an artery are made much smaller due to atherosclerosis, insufficient oxygen-rich blood is carried to that part of the body where the blockage occurs. Then that organ (or part of it) dies. Thus, if coronary arteries are blocked, the heart is not supplied enough oxygen-rich blood to sustain life and part, or all, of the heart muscle dies. If blockage occurs in the blood vessels to the brain, death occurs to that section of the brain deprived of oxygen. (This is called atherosclerotic brain infarction, the more common type of stroke.)

There are three major risk factors that compound one's chances of having a heart attack or stroke:

a. Hypertension—high blood pressure. The authors of the *Bostonia* article warn that the only way to tell whether you have hypertension is by having your blood pressure taken. Usually there are no symptoms of hypertension, which can be controlled through diet, drugs, and surgery. This condition needs constant monitoring for it is the most important risk-factor for heart attack and stroke.

b. Cholesterol. High levels of fats in the blood and blood vessels is a corresponding major risk factor in cardiovascular disease. A male aged thirty to thirty-nine has a four to five times greater risk of developing coronary heart disease if his cholesterol measures more than 260 milligrams than if it is below 200 milligrams. Wise diet measures and the changing of one's whole eating pattern can lower the cholesterol level.

c. Smoking—particularly *cigarette* smoking. This is yet another important risk factor.

If you smoke more than a pack a day you increase your risk of heart disease threefold. But you also increase your risk of lung cancer 23 times. Further, sudden death from heart attack occurs two to three times as often among men who smoke as among those who do not. Smoking is also the principal cause of emphysema, a disease that is rapidly becoming as great a health threat as lung cancer.[5]

Obviously the cure for this risk is to take the difficult step of stopping. The chances that one will die from a heart attack begin to decrease as soon as the person stops smoking.

Having one of these major risk factors doubles the possibility of heart attack or stroke. If one has two of the factors, the risk is quadrupled. And having all three risk factors increases the risk to more than eight times that of a person with none of these factors, as the chart on page 54 reveals.

The authors of the article note that there are other risk factors as well:

d. Diabetes.

e. Obesity. "Overweight people have more hypertension, more diabetes, and higher levels of cholesterol and fat in their blood. Extremely obese people have a markedly curtailed life expectancy."[6]

f. Physical activity. There is still controversy as to whether or not physical activity has a role in prevention of heart attack and stroke. At any rate, there seems to be clear evidence "that physical activity may help make a heart attack less severe by stimulating collateral circulation—blood flow in healthy vessels—which can compensate to some extent for blocked ones."[7]

There seems to be evidence that certain types of exercise can measurably improve one's heart's efficiency, enabling it to accomplish the same amount of work with less effort.

The kinds of activities that can accomplish these benefits are those

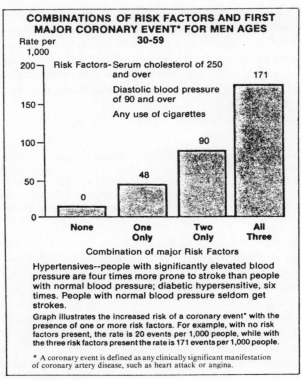

COMBINATIONS OF RISK FACTORS AND FIRST
MAJOR CORONARY EVENT* FOR MEN AGES
30-59

Rate per
1,000

Risk Factors-Serum cholesterol of 250 and over

Diastolic blood pressure of 90 and over

Any use of cigarettes

Combination of major Risk Factors

Hypertensives--people with significantly elevated blood pressure are four times more prone to stroke than people with normal blood pressure; diabetic hypersensitive, six times. People with normal blood pressure seldom get strokes.

Graph illustrates the increased risk of a coronary event* with the presence of one or more risk factors. For example, with no risk factors present, the rate is 20 events per 1,000 people, while with the three risk factors present the rate is 171 events per 1,000 people.

* A coronary event is defined as any clinically significant manifestation of coronary artery disease, such as heart attack or angina.

Bostonia, Winter, 1978, p. 4.

rhythmic exercises that use major muscles repeatedly, but at a steady level, below maximum capacity. They include such activities as jogging, running, swimming, and bicycling. If you do them regularly for sufficient periods of time, and neither too strenuously nor not vigorously enough, these activities produce specific physiological changes. Brisk walking, rowing, rope-skipping and running in place are among other exercises that can have the same "training effect" on your system.[8]

To have this benefit, such exercises should be performed at least three times a week, preferably more.

   g. Behavior type. Two California cardiologists, Myer Friedman and Ray H. Rosenman, investigated the correlation between personality types and heart disease. They arrived at a "Type A-Type B" behavior model and discovered that the typical "Type A" person suffers two to three times as much heart disease as the "Type B" person. The "Type B" person is rather relaxed, unhurried, and unruffled by life's emergencies and surprises.

The "Type A" personality has many of the following characteristics. If you are a Type A personality, it may be that you:

strive for more and more achievements, feel pressured and drive yourself hard . . . are aggressive . . . hasty, impatient, restless . . . dedicated to career goals to the exclusion of your family, friends and hobbies . . . have excessive motor energy . . . rapid speech . . . tense, tight smiles . . . can't relax . . . tend to drive, work and eat faster than other people . . . [are a] "workaholic" . . . conscientious, have high values and standards . . . try to beat records and crave recognition . . . like to do several things at once. . . .[9]

Dr. Meyer Friedman makes the following suggestions to help a person break the "Type A" personality pattern:

Discontinue polyphasic thinking. The habit of thinking about several things at one time produces a terrific mental struggle. . . .
Listen without interrupting. . . .
Read books that demand concentration. . . .
Have a retreat at home [a place at home where you can be alone]. . . .
Restructure trips and vacations. Avoid jam-packed, hectic [schedules]. . . .
Plan some idleness in every day.[10]

h. Salt appears to be an important factor in hypertension, although it is not yet precisely known how significant a factor it is. Quite probably Americans take in much more salt in their food than is needed.

i. Coffee and alcohol. Recent studies have shown that nonsmoking coffee drinkers showed no higher prevalence of cardiovascular disease than noncoffee drinkers. Alcohol in excessive amounts has many toxic effects on the body, including possible damage to heart muscle. On the other hand, there is nothing to indicate that "social drinking in moderation contributes to the development of cardiovascular disease." In one study, "those who consumed one to two ounces per day of hard liquor or its equivalent were found to have a lower risk of hypertension than either abstainers or heavy drinkers. . . . Thus it is possible to conclude that a single nightly cocktail might actually be therapeutic, but that anything in excess of that could be detrimental to your health."[11]

j. Genetic and environmental factors. While race and geography affect blood pressure levels, scientists have not clearly concluded whether that is due to differences in genetics, diet, or environment. There is some indication that job-related stress may contribute to the risk of hypertension. For example, a study of air traffic controllers, a highly stressful occupation, revealed that these persons had four times the rate of hypertension of the control group.[12]

Health and Cancer

The American Cancer Society suggests these seven safeguards with respect to cancer:

1. **Don't smoke cigarettes.** 30 million Americans have quit. They know it's the best way to prevent most lung cancer.
2. **Avoid overexposure to sun.** A broad-brimmed hat, a beach umbrella, protective lotion are ways to shield yourself.
3. **Monthly self-exam.** Monthly breast self-examination can detect cancer in an early curable stage.
4. **Exams regularly.** Your physician or dentist can easily detect mouth cancer. See them regularly.
5. **Pap test once a year.** Quick, simple, painless test which can detect uterine cancer before symptoms appear when the disease is most curable.
6. **Procto annually.** (Especially if after 40). The most common internal cancer. Highly curable if detected and treated early.
7. **Regular health checkup.** The most important safeguard. A complete checkup lets you know you are in good health.

They also urge all persons to know cancer's seven warning signals.

1. Change in bowel or bladder habits.
2. A sore that does not heal.
3. Unusual bleeding or discharge.
4. Thickening or lump in breast or elsewhere.
5. Indigestion or difficulty in swallowing.
6. Obvious change in wart or mole.
7. Nagging cough or hoarseness.

The Society advises you to see your doctor if you have any warning signal and points out that the cancer cure rate is up to one in three. It could be one in two if the disease were detected early and treated promptly. Therefore, they especially underline regular doctor's examinations and prompt ones when a symptom is noted.[13]

Health and Attitudes Toward Life

The above authors have offered us many guidelines that influence our health and increase our chances of vigor and survival into the later years. While we cannot live forever in these bodies, chances are that we *choose* to live longer or shorter in them; that is, we can improve our chances, though all of us know notable exceptions. The basic health question is, "Do I love and affirm life enough that I want to live longer and better?"

Eda LeShan cites evidence and theories that some mid-lifers purposely choose death rather than face life. Consider the story of a woman who is dying of cancer of the stomach. Seemingly, she has "everything to live for." A psychotherapist works with her and suggests there may be an alternative to dying if she can begin to examine her life. She responds, "I have no reason to get better, I am dead already." She tells the story of a rather subdued , suppressed life. In the midst of pursuing a hobby of photography, she found herself attracted to an older widower. She had an affair which she quickly terminated. Devastated by shock and guilt, she had trouble eating, and eventually she chose death.

Some persons told the researcher that death was preferable to the anguish of living. Said one, "I am fifty-six years old; every decision I've made has been a mistake since I was twenty-two. I don't have the courage or the will to begin again."

LeShan concludes, "If we want to stay alive we need to keep the body very much connected to head, to feelings, which influence our physical well-being to an absolutely staggering degree." [14]

Health and Stress

Therefore, in considering the subject of health, we need to explore the subjects of stress and personal attitude toward life. Some medical researchers feel these are the most important of all predictors of health or disease.

There has been a growing attention to the place of stress in a person's health. What is stress? "Stress is your body's physical, mental and chemical reactions to circumstances that frighten, excite, confuse, endanger or irritate you." [15]

Stress comes to us from many sources. The normal relationships of home, marriage, family, friendship, and work may produce stress. Changes in routine, even nice changes like vacations, weekends, and travel are tension producing. Interruptions in routine, such as promotions, changes in work, or moves from one community to another, produce stress. So do sickness in oneself or significant others, death, separation, and divorce. No one can avoid stress.

As Dr. Donald Oken points out, stress can be our friend or our foe.[16] Handled well, stress can be a friend that strengthens us for the next encounter which will surely come.

However, if stress is poorly handled, it can cause disease, such as "high blood pressure, ulcers, rheumatoid arthritis, asthma, or an overactive thyroid gland." Unbridled stress can also contribute heavily to heart disease and can have a part in weakening other organs in the body.

The term "psychosomatic illness" is expression of the fact that there are personal-social factors in every disease. But this term also indicates that emotional reactions play a major role in causing some of the diseases mentioned in the previous paragraph. "Many people seem to get [these diseases] only when they are psychologically stressed."[17]

Why are different people affected differently by stress? Why does one person escape illness, another get an ulcer, and another a heart attack? Dr. Oken responds that stress causes each individual to react with a particular emotion. (And your emotional response to the same circumstance may differ from mine.) "That emotional state affects certain body organs more than others. If the organ is a vulnerable one and the stress goes on and on, eventually, it will break down. Then you develop a disease in that organ. . . ."[18]

But it is possible that stress may contribute to even more serious diseases than those listed above. "Dr. O. Carl Simonton, a radiation oncologist and his wife, Stephanie Matthews-Simonton, a counselor and therapist, . . . have been exploring how stress and psychological factors affect both getting cancer and the course of the disease"[19] once it is contracted. While there is much that is not known, many studies indicate the probability that internal factors, such as attitudes, personality factors, stress management, and beliefs, play a role in susceptibility to cancer. The Simontons have discovered that one's psychological being and one's "sense of ableness" are powerful influences in the ability to deal with cancer.

Dr. Simonton relates the cases of two of his patients who had almost identical cases of lung cancer that had spread to the brain. One man had had the disease for over a year but had not missed work except for treatment. This man got in touch with what was most

meaningful in his life and began to spend more time with his family.
Simonton writes:

> I remember him saying one day, "You know I had forgotten that I didn't
> look at the trees. I hadn't been looking at the trees and the grass and the
> flowers for a long time and now I do that." It was interesting to watch him.
> Every week he improved, getting stronger, healthier.[20]

The other man stopped working and stayed at home watching
television all day long. He quit fishing, something he loved to do. He
watched the clock, yelling for his pain pills the moment they were due.
He died in a short period of time.

"The treatment for both patients was the same medically, the
diagnosis was the same, the patients' ages and physical conditions
were almost identical. The difference was in attitude, the way the
patients reacted once they knew the diagnosis."[21]

I'd Pick More Daisies

If I had my life to live over again, I'd try to make more mistakes next
time. I would relax. I would limber up. I would be sillier than I have
been this trip. I know of a very few things I would take seriously. I
would take more trips. I would climb more mountains, swim more
rivers and watch more sunsets. I would do more walking and looking, I
would eat more ice cream and less beans. I would have more actual
troubles and fewer imaginary ones. You see, I am one of those people
who lives prophylactically and sensibly and sanely hour after hour,
day after day. Oh, I've had my moments; and if I had it to do over again,
I'd have more of them. In fact, I'd try to have nothing else. Just
moments, one after another instead of living so many years ahead
each day. I have been one of those people who never go anywhere
without a thermometer, a hot water bottle, a gargle, a raincoat, aspirin,
and a parachute. If I had it to do over again, I would go places, do
things and travel lighter than I have.

If I had my life to live over, I would start barefooted earlier in the
spring and stay that way later in the fall. I would play hookey more, I
wouldn't make much good grades except by accident. I would ride on
more merry-go-rounds. I'd pick more daisies.

—Brother Jeremiah

Richard Nelson Bolles, *The Three Boxes of Life* (Berkeley, Calif.: Ten Speed Press,
1978), page 377. Used by special permission. Those desiring a copy of the complete
book for further reading may procure it from the publisher, Ten Speed Press, P.O. Box
7123, Berkeley, CA 94707.

If stress management is that important to health, how do you achieve stress management?

You begin by being aware of the stress in your life, by listening to your body and its pressures. Dr. Thomas H. Holmes and Dr. T. Stephenson Holmes have researched "How Change Can Make Us Ill."[22] They have discovered that persons are most susceptible to a variety of illnesses when they have been going through large, traumatic, or numerous changes in their lives. Out of their studies, they have listed some forty life events that involve change and have given them numerical value. For example, here are some of the number values: death of spouse—100; divorce—73; fired at work—47; change in residence—20; vacation—13; Christmas—12; etc.[23] They suggest if one's total score is less than 150, that person has less than a 10 percent chance of winding up in the hospital in the next year. If one's score is over 300, that person has a 90 percent chance of being hospitalized in the next year![24] So sensitivity to one's body, to one's experience, to one's needs is a vital first step.

Further, it would be good to take a second look at the advice for "Type A" personalities. The "Type A" personality is one who has not allowed oneself outward expression of emotion, and, therefore, the stress shows up in one's organs.

Next, learn to relax. Some of us live our lives so tensed up that, even when we "relax," our muscles are taut and our bodies filled with tension. We need to learn exercises which will help us relax, methods of meditation and achieving calm, and we need to take time out to be quiet and peaceful so that our body can claim its healing power.

Finally, we need to set a goal of holistic health for ourselves, for health is much more than simply a body function. I trust that this book presents to the reader possible alternatives for wholeness: meaningful career, including work, leisure and education; more sensitive relationships and enhanced self-concepts; growth opportunities and growth choices; conscious awareness of divine resources. There are so many exciting things to do and experience; it would be a shame to miss them for lack of a healthily maintained body!

You may wonder why I write a chapter on health and ignore the subject of menopause and metapause. The reason is that we are here addressing health decisions, while menopause-metapause, however experienced, is a health fact.

As has been noted, "Although eighty per cent of women have one or more symptoms which accompany menopause, only ten per cent have symptoms which interfere with daily routine, and after menopause, women have the easiest time in terms of physical and emotional symptomology."[25] If one experiences uncommon depression—anxiety, increased headaches and other pains, sudden experiences of heat and cold—she should, of course, consult with her doctor for help and relief. Menopause and metapause offer one more signal that the body is indeed frail and temporary. Therefore, its care and vigor deserve focused attention.

The Gospel and Health

If there is one thing that is abundantly clear, it is that our Master is with us in our search for health. He possessed an amazing compassion in the face of illness. He was a healer, and he wills health for us. But along with compassion and power, he brings us confrontation. As then, so now he asks, "Do you want to be healed?" (John 5:6*b*). Or to put it another way, "Do you prefer your bad habits (smoking, poor food choice, unhealthy mental-emotional attitudes) to health?" Do you want to be whole? If the answer is "yes," then the Master continues, "Rise, take up your pallet, and walk" (John 5:8). Our "yes" is that act of faith-trust that links our obedience to the power that can enable us to claim our wholeness.

I have been deeply touched by a modern-day telling of a person's discovering and claiming that power. In his book, *The Spirit of Synergy*,[26] L. Robert Keck tells of his own experience.

Physical overexertion, complicated by a childhood bout with polio, corrective surgery after a broken back, and a handball injury sent Keck into a deepening spiral of pain. Though doctors told him he would probably be permanently confined to a wheelchair, he found the power to triumph over unrelenting back pain through the use of medical hypnosis. After an exhaustive research based on his own experience and an intensive personal spiritual journey, he discovered some methods of harnessing mind/body/spirit or "synergy." These methods include a larger concept of meditative prayer than most of us have yet claimed. Keck subtitles his book, "God's Power and You."

Powerful resources are available to those of us who claim them and choose health.

"I will praise thee; for I am fearfully and wonderfully made;

marvellous are thy works; and that my soul knoweth right well" (Psalm 139:14, KJV).

Funny but true! (or too true to be funny?)
Middle age is:
—"the time when a man is always thinking that in a week or two he will feel as good as ever."—Don Marquis
—"(when you are too young to get on Social Security and too old to get another job.)"
—"when you're sitting at home on a Saturday night and the telephone rings and you hope it isn't for you."—Ogden Nash
—"(when you stop criticizing the older generation and start criticizing the younger one.)"
—"when your old classmates are so grey and wrinkled and bald they don't recognize you."—Bennett Cerf
—"when [you] are warned to slow down by a doctor instead of a policeman."—Sidney Brody
—"(when you want to see how long your car will last instead of how fast it will go.)"

From Laurence J. Peter, *Peter's Quotations* (New York: William Morrow & Co., Inc. 1977), p. 330.

5

WHAT ARE YOU GOING TO DO, NOW THAT YOU ARE GROWING UP?

Life Planning in the Mid-Years

One thing all persons in mid-life share is a need for reassessment. Basic questions emerge and demand consideration. Am I satisfied with my life the way it is? What childhood or youthful dreams have I yet to fulfill? Or modify? Or give up? What new dreams are occurring to me now? How do I recover my energy, my enthusiasm for anything? What do I deeply want to do before I die?

However, we come to these questions from such different experiences. Consider the following vignettes, all about persons in mid-life, all of whom face life-planning dilemmas:

If there was one thing clear to John, it was that his present position was a dead-end alley. His faithful work had been rewarded with periodic pay raises, but there had been no recent corresponding promotions. Many bright young adults had joined the firm since he, and some had already passed him. He had come to the point where work held no challenge for him. He could do his routine tasks without even thinking about them. How he hoped he did not become like Al, the notorious time waster down the aisle. Al had stragnated, had retired while still drawing a paycheck. But if he didn't like Al's option, what choice was there? Early retirement? That seemed like a copout, but what else was possible?

****

As she finished the breakfast dishes, Jane's mind went uneasily over the same questions that had been troubling her. Should she get a job? Part time or full time? What could she do? Where could she find work? Did the kids need her when they came home from school as much as she thought? Who would take over the Scout troop and church school class she'd possibly have to give up if she went to work? (There certainly seemed to be very few available volunteers around these days.) Would she earn enough to ease an overtight family budget? If she went to work, what would she gain and what would she lose?

****

"Jerry, you no longer fit into our plans. We're going to have to let you go." With those words from his supervisor ringing in his ears, Jerry walked out into a cold, crisp, autumn afternoon. How he dreaded the days ahead: facing the others at the office who would know he'd been sacked, looking for a new job. Who would want a fifty-one-year-old has-been? Still, he had to admit he felt just a little bit relieved. . . .

****

Julie had never guessed that such an offer would come her way. They had told her it was due to her excellent performance in her entry level jobs. Now she had received the offer of a position that had it all—attractive salary, recognition, travel, and great responsibilities. Still she felt just a bit hesitant. Did she want to enter that completely into a career? Would her marriage survive the strain? Was there enough marriage to be worth saving? Would there be time to pursue those interests that fed her spirit? Still, if you don't go ahead, you go back, don't you?

****

Jeff groaned aloud as he shifted through the monthly bills. "If I earn so much, how come I never have any money?" Really, he knew the answer. The big house, the new car, the kids' first-class college educations, their love of travel—somehow it all took more than he was making. The "goodies" at first had seemed a reward for his success. Though he tired of the pressure at work, he now seemed trapped by those very rewards. He reflected on the irony that while his success was envied by many people, his dominant feeling was fatigue and a longing for simpler days.

****

Recently bereaved, June asked herself again and again, "How does a forty-five-year-old widow, a college dropout, with no recent work history make a living?" For the last twenty-five years she had managed a household for herself, her husband, and their children. She had done so with love and efficiency. But now he was gone, and while his modest insurance policies would provide for her for a time, soon she must generate some income. At least she was not immediately thrown into the job market like one of her recently divorced friends had been. Still her dwindling bank account flashed warnings to her: go to work. But where should she go? What could she do? And how could she start?

****

All of these people have something in common. They all have need of thorough, thoughtful, systematic life planning. Quite possibly, you do too. However, before looking at the options before you and the methods you can use for deciding, take a look at where you have been.

Where You've Been

Gail Sheehy can help us at this point. Out of her interviews she divided the interviewees into several life-pattern groups. This is what she found.

Among males, there were three prevalent patterns. First, there were the *Transients* who were persons unable to make any firm commitments in their twenties, but who rather seemed to prolong the experiments of youth into their thirties. Second, there were the *Locked In,* who were persons who made solid commitments in their twenties. These commitments were often made without crisis or much self-examination. Thus, these commitments were often being questioned and perhaps overturned in the thirties or forties. The third group was the *Wunderkind,* the highly talented early achievers who created risks, played to win, and often believed that by reaching the top they would make all their personal insecurities go away. She also noted three other patterns less common: *Never-Married Men* (5 percent of males over 40), *Latency Boys* (who avoided the process of adolescence and remained bound to their mothers throughout adulthood), and *Paranurturers* (those who elected by occupational choice to care for the family of humankind, or to provide such nurturing—the kind usually provided by wives—to spouses and family). She discovered one further infrequent but emerging pattern among men, the *Integrators*. These were persons who wanted to be connected with life at many levels. They tried to balance their career ambitions with a commitment to families, and with conduct that is ethical and beneficial to society.[1]

Men, do you recognize yourself in her schema? Where do you fit? How do you feel about it? What implications for life planning does this recognition have? What would you like to change? To continue?

Among women, she found these life patterns. First, the *Caregiver*, a woman who married in her young adult years and at that time had no intention ever of leaving the domestic role. Second, the *Either-or-Woman* who in her twenties sensed she must choose between marriage, family, and children *or* work and career achievement. Sheehy sees two types here. The *Nurturer Who Defers Achievement*, like the Caregiver, postponed strenuous career efforts in order to marry and start a family. Unlike the Caregiver she intends to start a career at a later point. The *Achiever Who Defers Nurturing* postponed motherhood (possibly marriage also) in order to give preparation or career work priority. (In this connection, she also speaks of *Late-Baby Super Achievers*.) Then there is the *Integrator*, the woman who tried to combine and integrate marriage, career, and motherhood; *Never-Married Woman*, which might include the paranurturer (one who nurtures elsewhere as teacher, social worker, or as "office wife"—secretary); and the *Transient*, the woman who opted for impermanence in her twenties and continues to wander, occupationally, geographically, and sexually.[2]

Women, does her outline fit you at some point? Do you plan any change in the pattern? If so, what would you like to change? To continue?

Before leaving Sheehy's findings, it might be good to recall her observation that she gives more attention to women in the first half of her book and more attention to men in the latter half. This is because she observed more restrictions and inner contradictions on women during the first half of life, and more similar restrictions and difficulties for men in the second half.[3] If she is right, women, the saying may be true that life is beginning for you at forty. Men, we will have to be very wise and aware of what may happen if we don't want the second half of life to be a "downer" for us career-wise!

Not only changing life-styles but also other factors enter into the need for life-planning decisions at mid-life. Vivian McCoy, Carol Nalbandian, and Colleen Ryan identified the following reasons why mid-life persons came to them for career-planning workshops. Many people found that their first choice was inappropriate after trying it out. (Over half of college graduates end up in fields different from their major.) The inappropriate choice may have been made because of lack of knowledge about self or about occupational options.

Further, a person's interests may change over time. New research has indicated that all interests may not be inborn. Evidence suggests we can learn to develop new interests by exposing ourselves to new experiences.

Many adults also desire to grow and develop in their careers, even if they intend to stay in the same career path. Research has revealed that large numbers of men and women at mid-life have a desperate need to explore options and train for new occupations.

Further, later evidence challenges "the older myth that life provides us with only one appropriate occupational match." Vocational psychologist John Holland has done research to suggest "that an individual's combination of personal skills, interests, needs, and values may be reordered in new combinations to apply to a wide variety of fields."[4]

Where You're Going

What then are the options before you? Obviously, I must lay out these options in broad outline. Basically mid-lifers have four choices: (a) you can begin a career; (b) you can change a career; (c) you can seek career renewal; (d) you can engage in career reassessment and reevaluation.[5] Let's consider those options in turn.

a. You can initiate a career. My friend, Virginia Pipe, can speak to this issue from first-hand experience:

> While for males the issue at mid-life is career change, for many females the issue is likely to be career start-up. The energy devoted to rearing children can now be channeled into self-fulfillment through creative or volunteer activities, or a job or career outside the house and sensing of power that money and position bestows.
>
> Those of us who have volunteered for twenty years know that we have made our world a better quality place to live in. However, a first paycheck means far more to establish our worth in the eyes of society that does not value child rearing. However, we have hung in there doing our thing with children as a first career, because we chose to do so. In our semi-sheltered

world, however, we homemakers tend to underrate our own talents and abilities and managerial skills. We mistakenly think that anyone can run a household and guide the next generation in its development. And so we may need help in getting ready to launch a career.

Since my business partner and I floundered badly in our early forties in making the transition to careers, we felt we had something to offer from what we learned. And so, we designed a 24-hour-long class entitled "Is There Life After Children?" for homemakers who were approaching or in the empty nest. At the time we were completing our respective master's degrees, and the project was the final required paper for each of us.

The course starts off by helping women to answer the question "Who am I?" Homemakers may become submerged in the identities of others and may seek to fulfill themselves through husband or children. Also, children may have arrived on the scene before the mother's own identity formation was completed. In addition to forming a clearer self-portrait, the woman needs to build self-esteem, to rediscover interests set aside or neglected, to reassess values and reaffirm what they choose and own, to express their deepest needs, hopes, and longings. Then they need to screw up the courage to act on their newly affirmed identity and values.

This takes so much courage that I believe it is best done in groups of 8-12 rather than alone or in large groups. Women are powerful nurturers and can "mother" each other, caring sufficiently to confront gently. We have witnessed beautiful scenes of giving feedback, both positive and negative.

After having spent six to eight weeks building individual and group identity, the group could move into the Life Planning model suggested below.[6]

See section entitled "How Do You Decide What Option Is Right for You?" on page 70 for the life-planning model she refers to.

b. You can choose to change a career. According to experts, the average worker goes on a job hunt every three years. In this process a person may well change careers from three to five times in a lifetime![7]

At a recent conference on middle age, I heard the placement director for a large university assert, "Career change is incredibly easy, once you decide to do it. Most resistance to career change comes from inside a person, rather than outside." I was skeptical about that statement, frankly, because a career change I had desired to make (into higher education) had thus far proved impossible. And so I challenged him. He granted it was easier to change careers in some fields than others. Still, a majority of his clients did discover that once they were in touch with themselves and what they had to offer, they had more accessibility to career change than they had thought. (We will speak more about that getting in touch with yourself shortly.)

If you are seriously considering a career change, you might want to consider the advice from a recent *Business Week* magazine. To possible career changers they say:

—"Plan your move carefully," for it is a basic, vital change. They suggest that if you have not mulled it over for at least a year, you have not given it enough thought.

—"Assess your strong points" and match them against the strengths needed in the possible new career.

—"Consider your age." Surprisingly these writers suggest, "If you are over 50, sell it as an asset." They see job chances growing even better for older executives.

—"Be prepared for an emotional letdown" after you have made the switch. "When you change your career, you have to be patient. You won't recover all the confidence you had in your former career too quickly. It may take a year or two."[8]

c. You can seek career renewal. That is to say, you can choose to remain in the same general career area but seek renewal within it in many ways. For one thing, you can choose to specialize in certain parts of your career where you "really shine." As you hone those skills even more carefully, an old career can become a new challenge in which creative juices again begin to flow. Or, you can analyze what about your work conditions may be stifling your enjoyment and creativity. And then, quite possibly, you can negotiate the change of those job conditions which are stifling you. Or perhaps a new plan and discipline for continuing education can occasion renewal for you. Or, possibly, from your mid-career position you are ready to work for more systemic change in your field of work. You may choose to work toward making that employment pattern a more fulfilling experience for all who seek it.

d. You can engage in career reassessment and evaluation. Perhaps neither career change nor renewal seems possible. Possibly work has become dull and boring to the extreme. Still, you need not give in to despair and self-pity. Perhaps you can gain new appreciation that your work—dull though it may be—is important and basic for humankind. Perhaps you can discover other channels for meaningfulness. Possibly your contacts with persons at work give you opportunities to share love, caring, support, and a word of vital Christian witness. Perchance educational and leisure activities can be the place where you experience more significant meaning in life. Don't ignore the possibility that some volunteer activity—Big

Brothers or Sisters, Scouts, church school class or youth group, or whatever—can be an opportunity of fulfilling ministry for you. Perhaps you can plan an early retirement that can lead into a more meaningful retirement career. You may want to start making discoveries and taking the steps that make that possible. Even if your job has become a dead-end alley, life does not have to be!

How Do You Decide What Option Is Right for You?

Life Planning is much more effectively done in a skillfully led group. And so this will direct you to some possible ways of becoming a part of such a group.[9] In the meantime we will do the next best thing. I will share with you an outline of the basic questions you must answer. This is no casual construction. Rather, based on careful search and experimentation, it is Richard Bolles's discovery of what are the basic issues of Life/Work Planning.

Bolles has suggested that Life Planning may be visualized by thinking of a cart pulled by a *horse* down a *road*. The cart (or what's in the cart) stands for *what* you have to offer—that is, what skills, knowledges, values, and commitments. The horse suggests *where* you wish to use the skills you have—that is, to what you want to hook them. And the road suggests *how;* you need to learn *how* to identify the places where you would like to work, and then learn *how* to be hired in one of those places.[10]

And so you explore those questions. First, WHAT? What skills do you possess?

To help you answer that, consider some erroneous ideas that most people have about skills:

"First Erroneous Idea: *People are not born with skills; all skills*

Richard N. Bolles, *The Quick Job-Hunting Map, Advanced Version* (Berkeley, Calif.: Ten Speed Press, 1975). Copyright 1975 by Richard N. Bolles and the National Career Development Project. Used by special permission. Those desiring a copy of the complete book for further reading may procure it from the publisher, Ten Speed Press, P.O. Box 7123, Berkeley, CA 94707.

must be acquired." Not true. Some skills seem to be inborn.

Second Erroneous Idea: Skills are acquired primarily in school environments. The truth is many skills are picked up in home, at work, on the street, and in many places outside the classroom.

Third Erroneous Idea: You will be aware of the skills that you have. *Again untrue.* Persons use a wide range of skills often without the slightest awareness that they possess them. If one goes through a process of "skill identification," one may become aware of the considerable skills one possesses. (That workshop in which I wish I could lead you would spend much time on skill identification.)

Fourth Erroneous Idea: Skills are not transferable from one field or career to another. This is the biggest misconception of all. Many skills are abundantly transferable from one career to another.

Fifth Erroneous Idea: Individuals possess just a few skills and they probably are not marketable. This is again untrue, and it is sad that people so imagine themselves. The National Career Development Project has discovered that if a person will do skill identification, she or he will discover five hundred to seven hundred skills! The marketable combinations of these are endless.[11]

As you attempt to discover your skills, the following classification may be helpful. Vocational psychologists have discovered that we have three basic families of skills.

a. Self-Management Skills describe the way you manage life, get along with others, relate to space, impulses, etc. To speak of self-management skills is to describe your humor, tact, sensitivity, etc. For example, if you can get to work on time, take orders and criticism from the boss, work without supervision, dress appropriately, and get along with fellow workers, you have already demonstrated several valuable self-management skills. These are extremely important. It has been estimated that more people are fired for lack of self-management skills than for any other reason.

b. Functional Skills are those skills you have in regard to *information* (or data), *people,* and *things.* These are the abilities you have to do something or act upon something. And these skills are transferable. They exist across time. That is to say if you had a skill as a child, you still have it. It may be more sophisticated now or it may be long neglected, but it is still there. Functional skills that are used in one job may be used in many other jobs, roles, or careers. These are the skills that you need to recognize in yourself. Yet, at the same time, they are the hardest to recognize. These skills are so much a part of you that often you do them automatically.

    c. Work-Content Skills are skills using memory. These skills are acquired as you go through life. They are related to performing a job in a particular occupation, field, or profession (for example, knowledge of a foreign language, or of certain accounting procedures).[12]

    How do you discover your vast array of skills? The usual method in a workshop is very basic. You identify several "satisfying accomplishments" in your life—from any period of life, from any area of life, be it work, education, or leisure. Then you write a simple, sequential description of one of the accomplishments. Next you identify the skills you found there. Then two other persons also identify the skills in that accomplishment, for they will see the ones you missed. Finally, this information is recorded on a master grid of skills. In time your discovery of the range of skills you consistently used and enjoyed will amaze you and give you a most vital clue in life planning.

    In addition to these three types of skills, you need to ask other "What" questions. What goal, purpose, values do I wish to serve with my skills? Or, what is my philosophy of life, and how should it be expressed through work, leisure, and education? Or, what are those needs and causes in the world that really turn me on? What are those causes and needs to which I'd like to make some contribution with my life, no matter how small?

    These are the basic questions to ask in the "What" area: What skills and knowledges do you have that you enjoy using? What goals, purposes, and values do you wish to serve with them?

    Then you proceed to examine the "Where" question. This again breaks down into several other questions.

    What working conditions are important to you? You might begin to answer this by thinking of all the things that have annoyed you or irritated you in previous places of work. Then translate each of those from a negative quality that should be avoided to a positive quality that should be desired. Decide which of these are most important for you.

    What people environment do you desire? What qualities in people energize you? With what types of people do you find it interesting and enjoyable to work?

    But even more basically, what types of interests, skills, and values do you hope to find in the people with whom you associate?

Perhaps you can best get at this question by playing a little game. Here is an aerial view (from above) of a room where a party is taking place. Persons with similar interests have gathered in the same corner of the room as described:

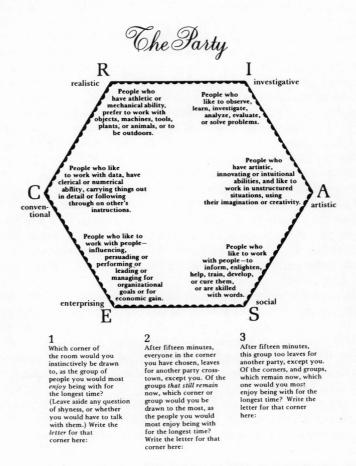

The Party

R realistic

People who have athletic or mechanical ability, prefer to work with objects, machines, tools, plants, or animals, or to be outdoors.

I investigative

People who like to observe, learn, investigate, analyze, evaluate, or solve problems.

C conventional

People who like to work with data, have clerical or numerical ability, carrying things out in detail or following through on other's instructions.

A artistic

People who have artistic, innovating or intuitional abilities, and like to work in unstructured situations, using their imagination or creativity.

E enterprising

People who like to work with people—influencing, persuading or performing or leading or managing for organizational goals or for economic gain.

S social

People who like to work with people—to inform, enlighten, help, train, develop, or cure them, or are skilled with words.

1
Which corner of the room would you instinctively be drawn to, as the group of people you would most *enjoy* being with for the longest time? (Leave aside any question of shyness, or whether you would have to talk with them.) Write the *letter* for that corner here:

2
After fifteen minutes, everyone in the corner you have chosen, leaves for another party cross-town, except you. Of the groups *that still remain* now, which corner or group would you be drawn to the most, as the people you would most enjoy being with for the longest time? Write the letter for that corner here:

3
After fifteen minutes, this group too leaves for another party, except you. Of the corners, and groups, which remain now, which one would you most enjoy being with for the longest time? Write the letter for that corner here:

Richard Bolles. *The Three Boxes of Life* (Berkeley: Ten Speed Press, 1978), p. 127. Used by special permission. Those desiring a copy of the complete book for further reading may procure it from the publisher, Ten Speed Press, P.O. Box 7123, Berkeley, CA 94707.

This little game corresponds with John L. Holland's highly respected research findings that people fall into six basic work personalities (or combinations thereof) for which there are six corresponding work environments (or combinations). Those three initials that you put at the bottom of the party exercise are a preliminary description of yourself and of the work environment you would most prefer. For example, if you wrote SAI, you are a social-artistic-investigative person and would prefer that work environment. If you wrote RCE, you are a realistic-conventional-enterprising person. That description of you can be verified or corrected through further vocational preference testing.

Another question to ask yourself is, "What level of responsibility do you want?" Or to put it another way, "What level of pay do you need?" How important is income to you at this point? What is the lowest salary on which you could survive? What salary would provide everything you would find enjoyable and important? How high is pay on your list of priorities? Can you afford to take a cut if other factors drew you into something that excited you?

And yet another question is, "Where geographically would you like to find this position?" If you have no strong preference, are there certain geographical qualities that would be important to you—such as climate, access to recreational or cultural facilities, size of community, nearness to (or distance from) certain members of your family?

Once you have answered all those questions for yourself, it is important that you put the information together in a way that you can visualize it. Perhaps, if you are of artistic bent, you will want to draw a flower (with one piece of information on each petal) or a house, or a car, or whatever. Here I'll just suggest a sentence completion outline. Giving yourself adequate space, complete the following statements:

I possess, use, and enjoy the following skills (self-management skills, functional skills, special knowledge skills). . . . . .

I would like to use these skills to serve these goals, purposes, values. . . . . .

With these preferred working conditions. . . . . .

In this preferred people-environment. . . . . .

At this level of responsibility and pay. . . . . .

At this location (geography wise). . . . . .[13]

Once you are equipped with this self-knowledge, and only then, are you ready to go on to the third major issue of life planning. *How* do you secure the appropriate position? There is a two-step strategy here. First you do a *Field Survey*. That is, you do a lot of talking, interviewing, investigating, and reading to discover possible positions that may include those elements you have learned are important for you. You begin by finding a person who holds a position that is similar to your self-description at any point.

You ask each such person you meet four basic questions: (*a*) How did you get into this field? (*b*) What do you like about it? (*c*) What do you dislike about it? (*d*) Who else do you know in the field? Who do you know who might be doing something even closer to my interests and needs as revealed on this sheet? (The last question is crucial.)

You continue this search until you are satisfied that you have located the type of work and (maybe even) the place where you would like to do it.

Then you research that place, discover what needs or problems they have that you could answer. Finally, you go to the person with authority to hire you, tell them why you are attracted to that place of work and what you have uniquely to offer them. And then have a plan B—that is another alternative in case that one doesn't work.[14]

It all sounds so simple and yet impossible at the same time. But I have talked with many of Bolles's clients for whom it worked. (And persons in my Life Planning groups tell similar stories!)

That is the Life Planning Workshop on paper I promised you. Now that you have read through it, go back to page 70 and spend time answering each of the questions about yourself. You may experience some surprises or some confirmations of hunches you have long had. Either way, it's a most worthwhile way to spend some time!

Here is that point in mid-life assessment where you need to spend the most time and energy. So much is at stake: you will be spending countless hours at work from now until retirement; you have opportunity to act on those beliefs and values which you cherish most deeply; and you have the challenge to make those mid-course corrections so that your remaining years will be a more appropriate "fit" between your individual uniqueness and your world.

Faith and Life Planning

The Christian faith speaks clearly and deeply about the use of life in the service of God who gave it. As one ponders the teachings of the Christian faith, there is a perspective on life planning. Specific guidance is offered as one ponders the "what" and the "how" of life planning. At least four faith concepts speak to the person about life planning.

First, the Bible teaches that each of us is a *steward* of all that God has entrusted to us. Everything we have and are is a temporary (and how we have pondered that word *temporary*) trust from God. Nothing is given us permanently. Our stewardship is called forth both in that God created us and in that Christ redeemed us and gave us gifts of the Spirit. The New Testament speaks again and again of the varied gifts that have been given to each of us. The most classic statement of this theme is Matthew 25:14-30, the parable of the talents. When the Bible speaks of talents, or gifts, these terms may translate directly to *skills* (all three kinds of which we spoke). The Bible makes clear that our God asks of us responsible stewardship (managership) of those marvelous five hundred to seven hundred skills that have been entrusted to us.

Second, the Bible makes clear that the life of the believer is to be one of *joy*. Did not our Master say, "I came that they may have life and have it abundantly . . . that my joy may be in you, and that your joy may be full" (John 10:10; 15:11)? Part (but admittedly not all) of *joy* is *enjoy*! Here is a vital theological clue about use of a life. Richard Bolles suggests there is a "Divine radar" in the discovery of *skills used and enjoyed.* He writes:

> . . . enjoyment, in human life, isn't a fluke. It's part of God's plan. He wants us to eat; therefore He designs us so that eating is enjoyable. . . . He wants us to procreate, love, and make love; therefore He designs us so that sex is enjoyable, and love even more so. *He gives us unique (or at least unusual) skills and talents; therefore He designs us so that, when we use these, they are enjoyable.*[15]

Third, the biblical concept of *calling* reminds us that God calls all of God's people, not just a selected few. A quick reading of the Bible leads one to discover that God called some individuals like Moses, Isaiah, Jeremiah, and others to specific tasks. Jesus called disciples. A more comprehensive reading reveals God called the whole people of Israel to servanthood. And Jesus called all who would follow him to repentance, discipleship, and service.

God's call is to the whole person, not just a tiny, private inward part called "spirit" or "soul." A whole person, a whole life-style, a comprehensive life of work, education, and leisure—that is what is touched when God calls a person to be a Christian.

The Protestant Reformers discovered this truth in 1 Corinthians 7:20, "Let every man abide in the same *calling* wherein he was called" (King James Version, italics added). Note that Paul uses the word "call" twice in the same sentence. The second "call" refers to a person's call to salvation. The first "call" refers to one's situation in life—married or single, slave or free, circumcised or not. From this passage the Reformers discovered that God calls all people, not just clergy. And God calls persons in all of their life, not just a part. To make this discovery does not make decisions any easier. But it does help one to know that one's present career may indeed be a calling (and thus have very special opportunities to serve God), and any future career option may also be a calling.

Fourth, the Bible contains the conviction that *God acts in history* and that, therefore, God calls you from the midst of history. This includes your personal history (your memory of where you've lived, what you've done, learned, discovered) and the larger history in which you live. In crucial times God calls out of history. God reveals a need to you and makes you aware of the resources available to meet that need.

These four items of faith—stewardship, joy, calling, and God-in-history—offer both perspective and specific guidance for the middle-ager's life planning.

Postscript
To those who are fed up, worn out, too tired to think about life planning and yet suspect they need it most.

(If that doesn't apply to you, skip this section).

Do you ever feel completely worn out, unenthusiastic, and drained in regard to your work? Do you say, "I've had it" or "I give up" or "I can't take it anymore"?

Then perhaps you are suffering from "burnout." What is "burnout"? The dictionary describes to burn out as "to cause to fail, wear out, or become exhausted by making excessive demands on energy, strength, or resources."

Students of the burn-out phenomenon note that it may show up in one's health and body, in such things as inability to shake a lingering cold, frequent headaches, sleeplessness, or shortness of breath.

But burnout shows up in one's behavior as well. Instant irritation and much frustration are signs. There may be suspicion, or paranoia. A person who may have been rather flexible in thinking becomes quite rigid, cynical—a closed book. The burnt-out one looks, acts, and feels depressed. One may spend a greater number of hours on the job, but accomplish less while one is there.

Who is apt to be a "burnout"? The dedicated and the committed who have great hopes and expectations . . . or those who have great demands of leadership and creativity placed upon them . . . and on the other extreme, those whose work is boring and repetitious.

Just as a person used to suffer through a mid-life crisis and think she or he was the only one who was enduring that, so persons also think that they alone are burn-out victims. Actually this problem is more widespread than is usually realized.

If one feels burned-out, should one change to a new and different career? Well, maybe, and maybe not. Probably a wise first step is to become aware of what burnout is and what it means. Read some more extensive literature about it. This note will direct you to such literature.[16] Then you might conscientiously take the steps that are suggested to prevent and to treat burnout. Some of those suggestions are: find more variety in the job tasks; if you have much close contact with people you serve, perhaps you need to reduce the contact time; work shorter hours at least for a while; perform directly contrasting activities, including much physical exercise in leisure time; create support groups among persons with similar tasks and problems; participate in possible educational experiences or workshops that may give refreshed insight and enthusiasm for your task.

But suppose you've tried to do some of these things, but just can't get any interest or enthusiasm for that old job? Then perhaps the time has come to pursue a new career. Do so, however, with one caution. Don't repeat the mistakes of the old job.

"Sure, I feel trapped. Why shouldn't I? Twenty-five years ago a dopey eighteen-year-old college kid made up *his* mind that *I* was going to be a dentist. So now here I am, a dentist. I'm stuck. What I want to know is, who told that kid he could decide what I was going to have to do for the rest of my life?"

Barbara Fried, *The Middle-Age Crisis* (New York: Harper & Row, Publishers, Inc., 1967), p. 59.

6

THE TOUGHEST CHALLENGE OF THE MIDDLE YEARS

Marriage for Middle-Agers

Eda LeShan has written, "There is no doubt whatever in my mind that the toughest challenge of the middle years has to do with love and marriage."[1]

LeShan is only stating an observation that is thoroughly shared by many students of middle-age marriage. I was surprised to discover how pessimistic most observers of middle-age marriage are about its prospects. While many mid-life marriages appear placid on the surface, treacherous currents rage beneath the surface.

It is noted that one-fourth of all marriages of fifteen years or more duration now end in divorce. In the last five years, divorce among couples married twenty years or more has doubled.[2] Some sociologists predict a tripling in the rate of divorces for mid-years couples over the next decade.[3]

For those whose marriages survive the divorce threat, there are ominous observations as well. Robert Blood and Donald Wolfe carried on a study in which they discovered that "in the first two years of marriage 52 percent of wives are very satisfied with their marriages and none notably dissatisfied. Twenty years later only 6 percent are still very satisfied, while 21 percent are conspicuously dissatisfied." They conclude that "corrosion is not too harsh a term for what happens to the average marriage in the course of time."[4]

Recently, I asked the leader of a seminar on "Middle Age Marriage" if the problems of middle-age marriage were that much different from other marriages. He replied, "I think so. Middle-age marriage tends to be more bitter. Middle-age marriage partners have more injustices and hurts to remember. And really, none of us ever forgets (or forgives) anything." His answer seemed overly pessimistic to me. Still, he was a psychiatrist reflecting on much marriage counseling experience.

Perhaps the above descriptions seem overly gloomy to you and they may be. But in truth, middle-age marriage has many problems with which to contend. These problems fall into three categories: (*a*) interpersonal dynamics (and thus common to all marriages); (*b*) intrapersonal dynamics of being middle aged; (*c*) institutions of society affecting marriage. Let's examine these in turn.

I. Interpersonal Dynamics

First, let us consider problems arising from interpersonal dynamics of marriage.

a. Lack of communication or *failure of communication.* Robert Lee and Marjorie Casebier write: "It is estimated that spouses miscommunicate 20 percent of the time, and that this faulty transaction wrecks marriages that might otherwise be workable."[5]

b. Mismanagement of conflict. George Bach and others have discovered the health-giving dynamic of openly facing and negotiating conflict.[6] But many marriages flounder because the partners ignore and deny the conflict that is inherent in any intimate relationship. On the other hand, those who recognize conflict too often use destructive rather than constructive techniques to deal with their problems.

c. Low time and energy *investment in marriage.* It has been estimated that husbands and wives spend, on the average, twenty minutes a week in conversation with each other alone! Marriages suffer from lack of attention. Indeed, there is one study that indicates that the most rapid deterioration in the marriage relationship is apt to occur in situations in which the husband has been most successful in his occupational pursuits.[7] The implication seems to be that the more one feels he must succeed and compete, the less attention he gives to the marriage relationship. Deterioration and dissatisfaction may soon follow.

II. Unique Middle-Age Marriage Problems

The fact of being middle aged can cause some "normal" marriage problems to intensify. The processes of aging contain the seeds of other possible marital problems, such as the following:

a. *Adult developmental crises* are *out of synchronization with each other.* We earlier noted how differently men and women typically come to the forties. Gail Sheehy has pointed out that these differences can contribute to marital conflict.

Up to this point in time, the wife may have been "piggy-backing" on her husband's dream, providing a tranquil home for him, caring for the children. But she is about to break out. She is going to seek her originality, creativity, her contribution outside the home.[8] At the same time, the husband may sense that he has gone about as far as he will, career-wise. His life is falling into a routine, and he is struggling to avoid stagnation. Reports Sheehy, "The most striking contrast between husband and wife in the mid-life couple is his sense of staleness compared with her usual feeling of unboundedness."[9]

One man's comment about his wife epitomizes this crisis:

... she's unbelievable now. She looks marvelous, she's found out she is still attractive to men, and it's all because she has found a whole new purpose in the world. I can't help feeling envious of her. Life seems so hard to me now; it's just the constant effort of keeping up. All I have to look forward to is writing another annual report.[10]

The wife may be startled to see her husband recognize his own weaknesses behind the masks of strength he has projected. The husband may be equally startled to see his wife as the emerging woman who will be resigning some old roles and taking on new ones.

Quite obviously, whether the couple stays together or not, this is the end of one marriage. If there is to be a new one, it will have to be renegotiated, with new roles for each.

b. The consequences of *both parents' overinvestment in* the *role* of *parent.* When children arrive in the home, many persons find this development to be an exciting and all-consuming opportunity. The result is that much attention and energy are given to parenthood. The problem is that this energy is diverted from being a marriage partner. As children become more independent, the results of neglect of the marital relationship may begin to be seen. Inevitably the time comes when children leave home. As a couple enter the "empty nest" period, they may experience a double grief. There is loneliness for the child who has grown up and left. But also, there is loneliness for each other because each partner is wrapped up in his or her own grief and has been out of touch with the partner's needs for quite some time. Or, the presence of children may have had a quite different impact.

c. *The consequences of one parent's overinvestment in the role of parent.* That is to say that with the birth of a child, a wife may put most of her psychic energy (that she had once devoted to her husband) into the child's needs. Or the husband may do so. James A. Peterson notes:

> In a conference recently a therapist remarked that he didn't know a case of middle-age divorce where the alienation had not started with the birth of the first child, the displacement of the father, his acting out in resentment, and the beginning of a long series of conflicts and tensions. He was exaggerating for effect, but the recitation given above is frequently repeated.[11]

Or the tension may be experienced in another way—

d. The *marriage caught between the generations.* In middle age, one is apt to have aging parents with unique needs and adolescent children also with very pressing individual needs. All in all, it makes for one more pressure for married middle-agers.

e. The *marriage in which one partner* has *"read the book."* Occasionally I counsel with someone who has become greatly excited over some book about marriage; for example, *Open Marriage; Love, Marriage and Trading Stamps;* or *Loving Free.* Or this person may have taken part in Transactional Analysis, or sensitivity training, or encounter groups. The only problem is that the person's marriage partner is not at all interested. This person finds oneself in a double bind. She or he is unhappy with the existing marriage and has a tool to improve the marriage. However, the all-important partner has no intention of entering that dialogue. This might be also described as the marriage where one partner grew and the other did not, or perhaps, more accurately, where partners grew at different rates and in different directions.

The uneven growth in different directions may also be in career development, volunteer activities, or attitudes about the aging process. If partners keep growing in different directions without reporting and sharing such information with each other, greater distance between them can be the only result.

f. *Marriage* as the *focus of the middle-age dilemma.* As the middle-aged person compares his or her youthful dreams to present reality, the marriage is part of life that may come under scrutiny. As the middle-ager redirects his or her course for the rest of life until death, he or she may ask, "Do I really want to continue this relationship?"

If either member is in that high emotional period usually called "mid-life crisis," he or she may answer this question in an overly pessimistic manner. One hopes that wider attention to the mid-life passage may make him or her aware that he or she has company in this moment. Quite possibly he or she may feel differently in time. He or she will be wise to avoid precipitous decisions about marriage during that time.

Or, to look at the same phenomenon from a slightly different perspective—

g. *Marriage* as the *result of the mid-life crisis.* Barbara Fried notes that "the capacity for intimacy depends on a firm sense of identity." Therefore when in middle-age crisis a person's sense of identity again wavers, a person's ability to sustain intimacy is reduced.[12] This withdrawal from the other may be necessary and quite possibly may be only temporary. But it is hazardous to the existing relationship and makes a person ever so susceptible to novelty in a new friendship or sexual partner. And, most dangerously, the person experiencing this will probably be quite unaware as to what is happening and why.

h. *The boring relationship.* Robert Lee and Marjorie Casebier note that the root word *bore* means "to make something empty," and they sense that many mid-life marriages suffer from this emptiness. Years ago Balzac warned, "Marriage must continually conquer the monster that devours, the monster of habit."[13] Lee and Casebier suspect this occurs in marriages when two people hold each other captive. Both become dissatisfied with the stimuli—the conversation, the shared experiences, the opportunities that are afforded in the marriage. "Habit, routine, sameness, emptiness, disenchantment, the feeling of being taken for granted, a blah feeling, a lack of any sense of value—all these are variations on the same theme."[14] They discovered that vital exchange of interests, feelings, and even conflict can interrupt the boredom routine and break the trap.

III. Strains on the Institution of Marriage

If the above problems were not enough, we face yet other difficulties in regard to the institution of marriage itself. Sociologists will tell you that a large number of marriages dissolve because the institution of marriage itself is in a state of strain. Nancy Mayer quotes a marriage counselor as saying, "I'm really not convinced that our pattern of marriage is a very good one for more than twenty years. Many people I see are really just dead on the vine. They live a pointless, meaningless kind of life."[15]

Many factors operate in our society that make it difficult to keep the lifetime commitment of our marriage vows in a meaningful way: We live longer so that the lifetime commitment is for more years. We usually live in cities at a distance from our extended family who usually are a conserving force in marriage and family life. We increasingly work in large industries at technical tasks that cut off contact from one's spouse and draw us into daily contact with a number of persons of both sexes who share our work triumphs and disappointments with us. The women's movement with its significant achievements has raised important, but troubling, questions about roles of men and women. We quite probably came to marriage with unrealistic expectations of marriage (which may have been unrealistically high or low) and with little or no explicit education for being an effective marriage partner.

Incidentally, About "The Affair" and Other Sex Matters—

A story is told about a couple who had been married for twenty years. One morning at breakfast both husband and wife were deeply engrossed in reading the newspaper. Suddenly the husband reached over to his unsuspecting wife and slapped her across the face, saying, "That's for being such a lousy lover." Then they went back to reading their papers. Suddenly the wife reached out and slapped her husband on the face and said, "That's for knowing the difference."[16]

This brings us to the subject of "The Affair" to which virtually every volume, whether on mid-life in general or mid-life marriage, gives considerable attention.

This literature reveals striking disagreements. Some estimate that more than half of all men and nearly half of all women in the mid-life age bracket have participated in an extramarital affair, while others set the figure much lower, suspecting that we are victims of a media hype. Therefore, they suggest, just like in the high-school locker room in our young days, we do more bragging than doing.

The literature disagrees on the motivations as well. (Of course, there may be many motivations so these may not be contradictions.)

—Some say middlescence is like adolescence, a time of assessing identity, which seems to be connected to sexual interest.

—Some say this is an attempt to deal with boredom in one's marriage and life.

—Some say this is an attempt to affirm oneself as attractive, even in the face of one's aging.

—Some say it is one's vulnerable way of seeking a simple solution when faced with the complicated, painful tangle of one's own marriage.

—Some say it needs no explanation. It is simply the result of relaxed norms and the increased contact between men and women in work, society, and business.

—etc., etc., etc.

For whatever reason, the affair may be both the symptom of marriage problems and the cause of one (unless the couple has a very explicit agreement).

In reporting this, I am simply attempting to be honest regarding the subject. This is a delicate marriage issue that cannot be ignored. Books have been written about this subject which we must treat very briefly. The majority advice seems quite clear—don't just drift and fall into an affair out of unconscious processes you do not recognize. Do think through the consequences which may include less fun, more responsibility, more involvement, and more pain than you had anticipated. If you are troubled about your marriage, honestly face that dilemma, rather than sliding into an affair.

Perhaps an affair has been your experience already, and you struggle with self-esteem and guilt. If so, I urge you to claim the forgiveness, grace, and new life that were available for you even before you asked. Too often Christians have assumed that sexual misconduct is *the* unforgiveable sin. That simply is not true. God's grace is available to us who fall short of the mark in this and every other area of life.

But if sex *outside* of marriage is receiving extra attention by one or both partners, some studies are showing that sex *within* marriage is lacking attention. In a recent study, it was revealed that 44 percent of married women between the ages of forty-five and sixty-five engaged in no sexual relations at all. The couples in the study agreed that in virtually all cases it was the husband's lack of interest that caused this to be so.[17]

All researchers reveal that physiologically nearly all men and women can continue to have and enjoy sexual relations into extremely old age. The research thus shows that a wealth of warmth and tenderness is available to mid-life couples who are willing to get in touch with each other and learn to love again.

Bad News and Good News

And so . . . if you felt a slight sense of unease about your marriage when starting this chapter, you may have concluded that the problem is not as bad as you thought. It is much worse! And that's the bad news.

The good news is that while achieving meaningful marriage in the middle years is difficult, it is not impossible. Persons will need to be aware, however, that a good, long-term marriage never just happens. It occurs because two people give it time, energy, understanding, and wisdom. Part of the wisdom is to seek help when it is needed.

James Peterson cites the case of John and Jean. One day when John came home (just four months after their last child had left for college), he found Jean crying. This surprised him because Jean had apparently made good plans to fill the void in her life. She intended to enroll in a writing class, renew relationships with friends her age, and take golf lessons so she could play with her husband. But none of this had worked out as she hoped, and with no sound in the house, there was an emotional void in her life she had not been able to fill. As she became more and more depressed, she could not hide it from her husband.

When John heard her sobbing, he took her in his arms, comforted her, and asked her what was wrong. As the story unfolded, he was patient and understanding. He took the next day off to take her for a drive. They spent time together, discovered spring flowers, and enjoyed each other. That week he canceled his appointment with his golf foursome to take her to a driving range and give her a personal golf lesson. On Sunday they stayed home, had a late breakfast, and spent the day talking about the years to come. Jean discovered her depression was gone. John's understanding of her feelings had buoyed her up. Peterson notes that as they continued to work on their relationship, five things seemed to account for the new spirit in their lives:

1. "They have achieved a *new intimacy*" and tenderness for each

other. They reinstituted middle-of-the-day phone calls, planned time for each other each week, learned how to laugh, love, and play.

2. "They learned to *intermingle their roles"* and share more of their life together. John again began drying dishes and Jean took over paying some of the bills. They planned yard work together so that they would have time for nine holes of golf or a drive at the end of the afternoon. There were no rigidly defined roles, no covert power struggles.

3. "They developed *a deeper relationship with friends."* They quite purposefully cultivated friendships where they sensed persons were in the same stage of life as they were. These friendships provided opportunity to replace some of the emotional investment they had previously given to their children.

4. "They achieved a *new relationship with their children.*" They learned to respect their married children's need for separateness, avoided criticizing or advising them, but filled their time with their married children with laughter and praise. When eventually their married children appeared to ask for advice, they handled it in adult to adult discussion. And so, their relationship changed from parent-child to friend-friend.

5. "They developed new and broader *avenues of service.*" Jean discovered an outlet for her parental love in work with spastic children; this in turn opened up opportunities in fund raising, leadership training, volunteer recruiting, as a part of broader service to the community.[18]

And so it was that a troubled middle-age marriage was renewed and flourished.

What of the rest of us? Is there a way for renewal of our marriages as well? If so, how do we achieve it?

To answer this question, I read widely, interviewed couples whose marriages were satisfying to them, and reflected on my own experience. I'd like to share three observations gained from this before going on to suggest some steps for revitalizing your marriage.

First, I share with you the insight of Ron and Marge. They suggested that a couple needs to marry, dis-marry, and re-marry many times in their life together. As I reflected on their marriage history, this made a lot of sense, for they had gone through more than their share of changes: early marriage, geographical separations, living in four different states, two families of children some twelve years apart, Marge's decision to go back to college in mid-life, and then her launching out on a demanding new career. Each of them has also grown as an individual, developed new interests and strengths, changed in many ways. How did they survive this and stay together with enthusiasm? Their backward reflection sees this process of "marrying, dis-marrying and re-marrying," occurring at intervals throughout their marriage. While some couples restate their wedding vows to each other every five years or so, and while Ron and Marge would affirm that and have done so on occasion, they are speaking of something more. They are talking about being free to change. They are able to sit down, terminate one type of marriage contract, and work through a new one, whenever this is needed. (Of course, there is much continuity from one marriage contract to the next; so this is not quite as radical as it sounds.) Their recommendation is "Marry, Dis-Marry, and Re-Marry."

Second, I share with you the experience of Lee and Barb. They suggest that daily communication is a must. Lee insists on at least a half hour every morning and a half hour every evening, and Barb heartily concurs. The half hour before Lee leaves for work they discuss business, schedule, finances, and plans for the day and coming days. In the evening, the communication is much more relaxed. They share the events of the day, their feelings, moods, problems—whether these problems are elsewhere or with each other. Even though they have been married for nearly twenty-five years, Barbara arranges a romantic, relaxed setting for this end-of-the-day conversation. This probably includes candlelight or a lighted fireplace, a delightful snack, or if Lee's day has been particularly hectic, a delicious, leisurely meal. And the hour may be amazingly late. However, both Lee and Barb find this pattern important in maintaining the meaningfulness of their marriage.

Third, I share with you a personal perspective on mid-life married love. My perception is that we need a new term (fairly secretive and vague), a new description, a new definition for married love in the mid-years.

My discovery of this came when I tried to find an anniversary card for my wife recently. I greatly enjoy greeting cards. Usually, with time, I can find just the right card with the appropriate expression for every occasion. But not this time. My only choice seemed to be either to avoid the subject with something meant to be funny, or give a card that spoke of our gloriously romantic, totally untroubled, unending, supportive marriage. That didn't fit us. (I seriously doubt if it fits younger married couples either, but we'll leave that for another time.)

What I needed was a card that celebrated our romantic, sexual relationship as pleasant and comfortable; that thanked her for making allowance for my weaknesses and failures as a husband, while I have not overly dwelt on hers as a wife; that communicated my appreciation for those many mundane things she does for me—like picking up on many chores uncomplainingly when my work pressures are great, helping me dress better than I know how, etc.; that stated my appreciation to her for her firm leadership with our daughters to whom I am gelatine; that recognized we had more differences than we realized when we married and have developed a number of extremely diverse interests now, but which celebrated our journey through life together. They don't make printed cards like that. And there is no language, no term that describes that incredibly complex mid-life married love.

Too late for that anniversary, I found the right kind of card. It was a photograph (my favorite medium) of a lovely rose (her favorite medium). Inside was blank paper for me to write whatever I wished. Maybe that's the way it ought to be with all anniversary cards, for as Barbeau reminds us, "Every marriage is a unique creation." [19]

Imagine a group of porcupines settling down to sleep on a cold winter night. Being warm-blooded creatures, they huddle together in search of mutual warmth. But the point inevitably is reached when sharp quills prick tender flesh, and they recoil away from each other. In this fashion they shuffle sleepily back and forth, back and forth, until they find a point of equilibrium at which they derive the maximum possible amount of warmth from each other, consistent with not pricking each other!

The porcupines illustrate very well the process by which two married people achieve a close relationship. We could call it mutual adaptation. It means strengthening the affinities and resolving, as far as possible, the hostilities. It is a difficult art calling for skill and patience. But it can be learned. . . .

David and Vera Mace, *We Can Have Better Marriages If We Really Want Them* (Nashville: Abingdon Press, 1974), p. 85.

How Do We Revitalize Our Marriage?

The first step to revitalization of marriage is *awareness*. Become aware. "What are the strengths of our marriage relationship?" Give this question careful thought. Enumerate the strengths to which you have become so accustomed that you take them for granted. Start with the question "What's right about our marriage?" Make a list of all the things you appreciate about your marriage partner. Have him or her do the same with you. Discuss with each other how your marriage feels when you have said those good things aloud to each other. Then go on and explore those aspects in which your marriage is not meeting important needs. Become aware of where your marriage relationship is giving you pain. Rather than minimizing your feelings about your marriage, become explicitly aware of its strengths and weaknesses. The above list may help you locate those points at which your marriage needs attention.

Second, make a *decision* about your *commitment* to your marriage. On one hand, your marriage may be so meaningful and satisfying to you that quite obviously you want to continue and grow in it. On the other hand, your marriage may have been a mistake from the start; your relationship may be filled with hurt and pain; you may feel that your marriage is dead. If so, your decision may be to terminate your marriage. (However, before you do, read some of the literature about divorce and talk with divorced friends. From my perspective, a decision for divorce is to trade one set of problems for another. Decide very carefully what set of problems you prefer.)

Or, your marriage relationship—like most—may fall somewhere between these two extremes. Perhaps your marriage does not provide a lot of personal support. If so, it might be wise to realize that most of the marriages in the history of humankind were marriages whose purpose was utilitarian rather than supportive. Until very recently, the definition of a "good marriage" would be one in which the children were raised, food and clothing provided, the tasks of farming completed. The idea that marriage should also provide a rich personal-emotional climate for deep sharing is a quite new thought! (So new that most of us have not become really good at implementing that thought!) We need to examine our relationship and come to a decision: how much do I value my marriage? Do I want it to continue? As it is? Or with significant changes?

Third (if you have so decided), make a *commitment* to the

renewing of your marriage covenant. As Christians, we have a special opportunity here. No longer are enduring marriages supported by society's pressures and culture's norms. Increasingly both of these work against lasting marriage. Therefore, building an enduring, meaningful marriage relationship is increasingly a challenging opportunity for those of explicit Christian commitment. (I am not judging those who find themselves divorced. Their challenges and dilemmas will be discussed shortly.)

Fourth, find a way to *implement* your commitment. Perhaps you can follow the example of John and Jean cited above. Possibly you can plan time to do those things that would enhance your relationship. You may want to stimulate your thought by reading and discussing books on marriage either as a couple or a group of couples. You might be able to recruit your pastor or some other skilled group leader to lead such a group. I will suggest possible resources for such a group at the end of this book. It might be that you would want to consider a Marriage Enrichment experience of some sort. This note will direct you to resources for enriching your marriage.[20]

If your partner chooses to avoid such experiences, you have the more difficult task. It's impossible to counsel half a marriage, and it's most difficult to build half a marriage! Still, it is possible to create new attitudes within yourself and, thus, a different climate in your marriage whether your partner is interested in changing or not. Perhaps you need to apply to your marriage the well-known prayer, "Lord, give me the courage to change the things that can be changed, the serenity to accept the things that cannot be changed, and the wisdom to know the difference."

Eda LeShan was right! Some of the great challenges of mid-life are in the realm of love and marriage. But for those willing to take the risk, possibilities of hope and renewal lure us on.

(The fifth perspective on marriage will be given at the end of the next chapter.)

7

SINGLENESS AND REMARRIAGE

Alternative Life-Styles for Middle-Agers

Increasingly people in mid-life are experiencing two alternatives to lifelong marriage. Some are single. Some remarry. The dilemmas facing these persons deserve attention as well. Sadly, neither I nor many other mid-life observers know much about these life-styles. But we shall start and attempt to understand. Perhaps consciousness and empathy can be raised.

Singleness

When one thinks of it, it is strange how little attention we pay to the subject of "singleness."

There are, of course, three "routes" to singleness. Some of us have never left the unmarried state. Some of us have become single because of the death of a spouse (an event that takes a disturbing upturn in frequency and will touch more and more of us in coming years). Others will become single by means of divorce, a fast-growing phenomenon among all married people, including mid-lifers. For some, mid-life singleness will be a permanent condition and for others a temporary status while making the transition to a new marriage.

Therefore, *every one of us who survives will be single for some portion of the remainder of our lives.* Indeed, a recent study showed that 85 percent of women ages thirty-four to fifty-nine can expect to be a displaced homemaker for some time during that period. And those of us who precede our spouses in death have a real stake in that person's happiness and welfare as a single. This subject deserves much more careful and detailed attention than I will be able to give here. Perhaps at least we can begin to be more aware.

Most of the mid-life singles will become single by the routes of divorce or death. Though both widows and widowers and divorcées and divorced men sometimes resent the comparison, the early experience of both has a good deal of similarity. The first stage is a time of grief. There is possible preoccupation with the person you lost, a continual recalling of the events that led up to the loss and the circumstances surrounding it. There are attempts to make sense out of things and, at times, an overwhelming numbness. Adeline McConnell recalls her first grief experience as accurately fitting a description of grief she'd heard somewhere "as a slide into a bowl, a slide that levels out at the bottom before the climb out can begin." [1]

Following the numbness, there are likely to be the strong twin emotions of anger and guilt. These emotions may ebb and flow but are an important part of a growing realization and acceptance of a real loss in life.

McConnell and Anderson summarize:

> Most of the new singles—widowed, divorced, or separated—had to cope with their agony, deliberately or instinctively, reviewing the circumstances of their bereavement over and over, making sense out of it and finally integrating it into a new view of the world. Adjusting to the new life they were to build for themselves, they would gain new insights, new strengths, new emotional maturity, until they became, like a healed fracture, stronger than they were before. [2]

But then comes another stage of grief, depression. Some psychologists believe depression must run its course, like the common cold.

While these stages are inescapable, one needs to avoid the temptation to "lock into" them and never move beyond them. Admittedly this is glib, too quick advice. If you find yourself locked in any stage of grief and unable to break out, I urge you to seek professional help. In time, one will need to claim energy, to make decisions about one's life, and to take charge of life again.

As one rearranges one's "inner furniture," veteran singles advise the rookies to give attention to two parallel concerns: to learn to be good to oneself by choosing whatever experiences, activities, and purchases that will bring pleasure and remind you that you are a worthwhile person; to face the issue of loneliness, which is one of the greatest problems that many single people face. Loneliness can be dealt with, they say, both without and within. One is most wise to anticipate when some of the most lonely times will be and plan activities for companionship for those times whenever possible. As for the inner loneliness, dealing with one's self-esteem and happiness and discovering those treasured activities that you can only do alone may help one cope on that level.

In time, the single must build a new life-style and structure. This may well include a changed work pattern and a changed income pattern. It will certainly involve a changed status, since "married" and "single" are quite different statuses in our society. Further, a spouse may well have derived such identity from association with husband/wife, and that "derived identity" is now gone. Many new singles are amazed to see old friendships with couples quickly fading, for the new single may be seen as a threat. The single may be seen as competition for attention of married persons of the opposite sex, or she or he may be one who causes discomfort and experiences discomfort in the same circles that were once so familiar.

It becomes quite apparent that one's social life as a single will shrivel considerably if one does not take steps to expand it beyond the circle one had as a married person. But for those who are courageous enough to reach out and patient enough to keep trying, there are growing opportunities for singles to build a satisfying social life and support system.

Churches are increasingly developing ministries with single people. Parents Without Partners and a number of other groups offer opportunities to deal with mutual interests and problems while meeting persons who share these concerns. And nearly every worthwhile interesting activity (adult education, community recreation groups, etc.,) has increasing numbers of singles as participants.

In time the single person will need to examine whether she or he prefers singleness as an enduring status or whether a new marriage should be investigated. Most observers encourage that this decision not be made in haste. One should avoid precipitously "leaping" before "looking" simply to escape the terror of being alone. For quite possibly, that alone state has much to commend it to some persons.

The sudden advent of "singleness" causes a new, urgent episode of that self-identity seeking that we noted is common to all mid-lifers. From a new perch in life, one asks anew: Who am I? What do I want to do? To be? To contribute in life? Can I do this best as a single with the support of friends and acquaintances? Or do I prefer to be married? What would I gain, and what would I lose if I were married (specifically married to the person under consideration)?

In making the decision of whether or not to marry, McConnell and Anderson advise caution. They laughingly recall an interview with one of the country's leading authorities on aging. At the end of the interview, she spoke to them "from her vantage point of her forty years of marriage: 'I predict you will remarry. You both seem to have a *lot* going for you.'"[3] As the intent of her comment sunk in, they burst out laughing. "It sounded as if she thought singleness was a condition to be recovered from, while we regarded it as a lifestyle to be enjoyed."[4]

They suggest that instead of being second-class citizens, singles can claim a life-style with dignity and beauty. They reflect on their own experience, and that of the many middle-aged singles they interviewed for their book, and say that these people

. . . have put together a new lifestyle which is part of an influential new cultural pattern on the American scene. Instead of hovering around the periphery of the coupled culture, to babysit grandchildren or be charitably invited for Christmas dinner, they have become pioneers, blazing a trail— like all pioneers—in their own self-interest. With a longer lease on youth and vitality than people have ever enjoyed before, they are focusing the wisdom and experience acquired over half a century on the last two decades of life, to make them effective, creative, vigorous years. In so doing, they are making the world take another look at a double stereotype: the person who is older and who is single as well.

By their self-dependence, by their freedom, by their very happiness, they are saying that it's okay to be single, it's okay to be older; that it is, in fact, a very good time and state in which to be alive.[5]

Reconstituted Marriages and Families

Though remaining single may be a good option for some, statistics show that four out of five divorced persons remarry eventually. (On the average, persons remarry three years after the termination of their former marriage.) Brenda Maddox estimates that every year in the

United States nearly one million children under the age of eighteen see a parent remarry, and over half a million adults thus become stepparents. Roughly one in every eight children in America is a stepchild.[6]

Though remarrying and forming new family constellations is a growing pattern, far too little attention has been given to the unique problems and, hence, unique insights and skills that are needed to be successful in this venture.

One new stepparent put it this way, "It's like being plunked down, a stranger, in the middle of rural China, speaking the wrong language and yet torn all the while by too many people asking unanswerable questions."[7] Or, as another new stepparent described it, marrying into a new family is like trying to learn to swim in the deep end of the pool rather than the shallow end!

Remarried parents testify that while they had thought it would be so simple ("I love you, I'll love your children"), it never proved to be as simple as they had anticipated.

To begin with, newly remarried couples have nearly all the issues mentioned early in chapter 6 to contend with as do all other married couples. Oh, they escape a few of those issues. They don't deal with accumulated resentments nor the possible boredom of a long-term marriage. They begin with the energy that comes from a new commitment to each other.

But they face a myriad of issues that once-married couples don't. I have often seen persons choose a new spouse more wisely the second time and develop the relationship with more sensitivity and promise than they did in their first marriage. But then, as the couple moves into marriage, they become drawn into a tangled network of personal relationships that call for more human relations skills than they have.

To begin with, there are too many people in a second marriage. Consider recently married Phil's statement:

> "I didn't marry my wife, I married a crowd. . . . There are my three sons, who give me the silent treatment when they see me every other weekend, *and* the twin ten-year-old daughters of my new wife, Carolyn, who frankly are often a pain . . . *and* my new in-laws, who cold-shoulder me, *and* Carolyn's ex-husband, who spoils the twins rotten when he sees them, *and* my ex-wife, who is still bad-mouthing me to my kids, *and* the Bank of America's Credit and Loan Department."[8]

Second, there are apt to be financial problems. Child support payments and/or housing large enough to put a roof over the new, reconstituted family unit quite probably will put a strain on existing finances. Even if there is enough money, financial arrangements can be complicated and troubling. In thinking of his assets and estate, what does a man owe to the children of his former marriage? If money is a scarce commodity, how is it decided who gets the teeth braces? The summer camp? Private lessons?

Third, each marriage partner may experience an unconscious resentment of the other's children. There may be a quite simple reason. The children are reminders that the spouse loved someone else previously. As observers put it, a second wife or husband is always second! (Then, of course, there may be disagreeable behavior on the part of the children that encourages this resentment to build.)

Fourth, there is apt to be much confusion about identity and responsibilities in the step-family. By contrast, in the original family we all know what a father or mother is and what we should call each other. But what is a stepmother? A stepfather? How do stepparents introduce stepchildren and vice versa? What do they call each other? What do they expect of each other? What do they need from each other? Maddox notes, "The clarity of family life is absent in stepfamilies and undefined relationships in close quarters do not make for easy living."[9]

Stepmothers probably typically feel this vagueness the most strongly. Ruth Roosevelt writes: ". . . I, for one, had trouble understanding the requirements and limits of my role [of stepmother]. I could take the limits without the responsibilities, or the responsibilities without the limits. But both together?"[10] She speaks of responsibilities—cooking for six or more, purchasing, sewing, washing, cleaning, taxiing—as well as crises to deal with. She says it looked like mothering. But then the stepchildren, when away at summer camp, sent letters to the father's office, not to both of them. On a vacation trip, the children would express the wish that their "real" mom were going along. She reflects: "I find it hard to accept the limits. A stepmother is not, repeat, is not a mother. But she sure is something. The question is always how much or how little of that something is she?"[11]

Typically the stepfather has a frustration as well. He may well find himself fathering another's children while his own are not with him.

He winds up doing for other children what he is not able to do for his own.[12] But even with another's children, the same ambiguity prevails. A stepfather is not a father, but what is he?

Fifth, children may well have problems that intensify the marriage problem. For they quite possibly now spend time with two original parents and two stepparents—their parents' new spouses. There may be tension; there will at least certainly be some inconsistency between the two couples' life-style and discipline of children. Children will detect these inconsistencies, capitalize upon those differences, and become quite confused as to what is actually expected of them. This tied to any other resentments or insecurities the child feels in the new household arrangement can lead to a series of behavioral crises that strain the new marriage even more.

In short, if persons need to be courageous to launch a first marriage, they need to be doubly so to begin a second one!

Mel Krantzler offers the following Creative-Commitment Guidelines for those entering a marriage in which they will be stepparents:

First, *"Prepare the way for the new family relationship before your remarriage."* Give the children time to absorb this news. Help answer their questions about what this means for them.

Second, *"Respect the readiness time of children to adjust to the new family environment."* Quite probably, he says, this will move through four stages. Stage one: you are the stranger who may be seen as the one who might "take away" the children's parents' love for them; stage two: you become a tolerable acquaintance; stage three: you become a friend in whom increasing trust can be placed; stage four: you may become a good and loved friend, but the stepparent will rarely or ever become a loved parent.

Third, *"Create an accepting environment for the children."* Listen a lot. Don't ask for the affection that they can give only their real parents. Through actions make the offer of friendship.

Finally, *"Be honest with your feelings."* There needs to be mutual sharing of pain, confusion, anger. Only if this is done will the vague relationships of the new household come into workable focus.[13]

Faith and Marriage—Singleness—Remarriage

What is the gospel for this aspect of life, for marrieds and singles? The gospel begins with the proclamation that each of us (male and female) is created in the image of God, loved and cared for by God.

Therefore each individual is complete. The person does not need marriage to become a complete person. Singleness is an acceptable (and sometimes particularly blessed) state before God. (It is high time for the church to follow the gospel rather than culture's assumptions on this subject.)

Further, the gospel affirms that the loving relationship between husband and wife exists within the very creative purposes of God. From Genesis 2: The man beholds the woman and exclaims with delight, "This at last is bone of my bones and flesh of my flesh." And the passage concludes, "Therefore, a man leaves his father and his mother and cleaves to his wife, and they become one flesh" (Genesis 2:23-24). That simple phrase, "one flesh," holds forth a magnificent possibility for married people. It is that a continued and growing covenant between two people before God can lead to a dynamic process of shared personhood, a new reality that is greater than the former.

This deep spiritual unity between man and woman is clearly intended within Bible passages to be a permanent union. When two persons fail to keep that commitment and the marriage fails, there is both sin and tragedy. The rocketing divorce and remarriage rate reported in this chapter is sadly and regretfully reported. There is much brokenness here. Somehow, in the turbulence of our society these days, we have not held high enough the claims and possibilities of Christian marriage, nor have we equipped ourselves for meaningful, lasting marriage. We all have much for which to repent.

But the gospel affirms that when we repent, God touches us with grace. Divorce and remarriage is a failure of covenant; as such, it is sin. However, it is not THE sin. The same forgiveness, redemption, and rebirth that are available for any others who fail are available for the divorced and the remarried.

Myrna and Robert Kysar see remarriage as a possible sign of resurrection and new life.

> The poignant symbols of death and resurrection are applicable here. The first marriage is dead, and with it have died the hopes and dreams of the individuals involved. But there may be a resurrection. God brings life out of the death of marriage. That life may take the form of remarriage. The church . . . has at its disposal a powerful set of symbols by which to support the divorced person's desire to start again in a marriage relationship.[14]

Finally, the gospel reminds us that people and people's actions can be signs of God's grace in our midst. "Let all bitterness and wrath and anger and clamor and slander be put away from you, with all malice, and be kind to one another, tenderhearted, forgiving one another, as God in Christ forgave you. . . . And walk in love, as Christ loved us . . ." (Ephesians 4:31-32; 5:2). Though we may well have been hurt in relationship, so can we be restored. Scripture reminds us that when people restore us in love, it is God who is doing the healing.

8
THE MIDDLE GENERATION
The Mid-Life Person as Parent and Child

As a middle-ager, I have some other relationships to renegotiate in addition to my relationship to my spouse.

For I am not only in the midst of life, but I am also in the middle of three generations. As a middle generation person I may be caught in a tension that pulls both ways. I believe it was Margaret Mead who suggested there is a reason that young people and their grandparents get along so well together—they have a common enemy! That may be putting the matter too strongly. Still, I am the parent of children; I am the child of parents. Both relationships are in a state of flux in mid-life. Let's take a look at each in turn.

The Mid-Life Parent

Since our possible childbearing years extend over at least three decades, mid-life parents have children of a wide variety of ages. Thus, a mid-life parent may find him or herself at a PTA with other parents half his or her age. Most typically, however, mid-life parents have children who are in their teens and twenties. Since parenting of persons in this stage of life seems particularly confusing, I will concentrate my attention there.

To begin, let's take a brief glimpse at the experience of a rather famous mid-life parent, Erma Bombeck, in "You Don't Love Me":

"You don't love me!"

How many times have your kids laid that one on you?

And how many times have you, as a parent, resisted the urge to tell them how much?

Someday, when my children are old enough to understand the logic that motivates a mother, I'll tell them.

I loved you enough to bug you about where you were going, with whom, and what time you would get home.

I loved you enough to insist you buy a bike with your own money that we could afford and you couldn't.

I loved you enough to be silent and let you discover your hand-picked friend was a creep.

I loved you enough to make you return a Milky Way with a bite out of it to a drugstore and confess, "I stole this."

I loved you enough to stand over you for two hours while you cleaned your bedroom, a job that would have taken me fifteen minutes.

I loved you enough to say, "Yes, you can go to Disney World on Mother's Day."

I loved you enough to let you see anger, disappointment, disgust and tears in my eyes.

I loved you enough not to make excuses for your lack of respect or your bad manners.

I loved you enough to admit that I was wrong and ask your forgiveness.

I loved you enough to ignore "what every other mother" did or said.

I loved you enough to let you stumble, fall, hurt and fail.

I loved you enough to let you assume the responsibility for your own actions, at six, ten, or sixteen.

I loved you enough to figure you would lie about the party being chaperoned, but forgave you for it . . . after discovering I was right.

I loved you enough to shove you off my lap, let go of your hand, be mute to your pleas . . . so that you had to stand alone.

I loved you enough to accept you for what you are, not what I wanted you to be.

But most of all, I loved you enough to say no when you hated me for it. That was the hardest part of all.[1]

Adolescence is . . .

What is it that makes parenting adolescents such a delicate and difficult task? Let's take a brief look at this process from several vantage points.

First, it is helpful to remind oneself of the tremendous and turbulent changes that take place in a person during adolescence.

Years ago, Evelyn Duvall listed the basic developmental tasks of teenagers—those tasks one must accomplish during these years if one is to be ready for the next stage of life. She suggested the following:

1. *Accepting one's changing body and learning to use it effectively;*
2. *Achieving a satisfying and socially accepted masculine or feminine role;*
3. *Finding oneself as a member of one's own generation in more mature relations with one's agemates;*
4. *Achieving emotional independence of parents and other adults;*
5. *Selecting and preparing for an occupation and economic independence;*
6. *Preparing for marriage and family life;*
7. *Developing intellectual skills and social sensitivities necessary for civic competence;*
8, *Developing a workable philosophy of life that makes sense in today's world.*[2]

Though the content of some of those developmental tasks changes from generation to generation, still the above list forms a good summary of what a teenager must accomplish in a few short years of time.

The central theme in all these tasks for teenagers is the search for identity. This identity is different from one's childhood identity and is also different from one's parent's and family identity. It can only be discovered and claimed through experimentation, through trial and error. And therein lies much of the turbulence between teenage children and middle-aged parents. Haim Ginott suggests "Adolescence is a period of curative madness, in which every teenager has to remake his personality. He has to free himself from childhood ties with parents, establish new identification with peers, and find his own identity."[3] Ginott suggests further that the purpose of adolescence is to "loosen personality." The adolescent's personality is undergoing the required changes from the organization of childhood through the disorganization of adolescence to the reorganization of adulthood.[4]

In describing this search, Ginott aptly reminds us, "Adolescence cannot be a perpetually happy time. It is a time for uncertainty, self-doubt, and suffering. This is the age of cosmic yearnings and private passions, of social concerns and personal agony."[5]

Anna Freud suggests:

> It is normal for an adolescent to behave in an inconsistent and unpredictable manner; to fight his impulses and to accept them; to love his parents and to hate them; to be deeply ashamed to acknowledge his mother before others and, unexpectedly, to desire heart-to-heart talks with her; to thrive on imitation of and identification with others while searching unceasingly for his own identity; to be more idealistic, artistic, generous, and unselfish than he will ever be again, but also the opposite: self-centered, egoistic, calculating.[6]

She points out that such fluctuations would be considered abnormal at any other time of life. But during adolescence these drastic changes are but the signs of an adult personality structure slowly being constructed while the person is keeping all options open!

While it is relatively simple to describe adolescence in clinical terms, it is not nearly as simple to live with it. By definition it is quite possible the adolescent may well

—be so considerate of friends while being a downright rat to brothers and sisters.

—express love to parents in "mushy" terms and then selfishly ignore one's own fair share in all household tasks.

—reject cherished values of parents (for example, loyalty to church) as hypocritical while blindly practicing a judgmental hypocrisy of one's own.

—take risks with cars and cycles resulting in near injuries or actual ones.

—experiment with alcohol and other drugs, sex, independence, etc.

—give a public speech in which she impresses all with her maturity and then throws a temper tantrum in a clothing store over a dress that doesn't fit.

—be beautiful and feel ugly; be talented and feel worthless.

The scholars may be right. The adult personality may emerge from the adolescent in time. But how painful the wait! And we mid-life parents do the waiting.

(In order to make a point, I am overstating this. I should hasten to add some teenage persons seem to achieve their adult identity with a minimum of storm and stress. Obviously not all adolescents fit the same mold here. I cannot explain the variation. My only purpose is to point out that adolescent turbulence is natural and not necessarily failure on the part of either parent or child.)

Changes That Influence Family Life

Second, we note some changes in our world that complicate our parenting tasks.

Consider the change in family function that has taken place over the last century. Kenneth Keniston and the Carnegie Council on Children note that most present literature on the family is based on two false assumptions: (*a*) "that parents alone are responsible for what becomes of their children"; (*b*) "that families are free-standing, independent and autonomous units, relatively free from social pressures."[7] Keniston suggests that assuming these two incorrect myths blinds us to the forces that are operating in family life today.

There was a grain of truth to these assumptions a century and a half ago when most American families were largely self-sufficient farmers. The whole family worked together to produce what the family needed; this family was taught and directed by father and mother. Children were useful economically, for each person did much vital work to produce the food and clothing.

For most, this pattern has drastically changed. Children are no longer an economic asset. Rather they are an economic drain. A conservative estimate is that the total cost of housing, feeding, and clothing one child through high school now totals $35,000. Then comes the cost of post-high school education.

A second change is the removal of the responsibility for education from the family. In the early nineteenth century most education occurred in the home. Now, for fourteen to sixteen years the American child spends the better part of most weekdays in the presence of day-care workers, teachers, and other children the same age. (There is also another important "teacher" of our children. By age eighteen, the average American child has spent more time watching television than he or she has spent in school or with parents.)

A third change has been in the care of the sick. Even a century ago, most care of the sick was a family matter. Much as we are happy for skilled doctors, available hospitals, and all, unfortunately the family plays a diminished role in health care.

The family's role in communicating values and faith, in caring for aged members, in supporting one another when someone is out of work or in other crises—these functions have diminished as well.

While family functions have been decreasing, we are also experiencing rising expectations as to what we want to give our children. Parents have to search for the best possible education for their child, for corrective or compensatory programs if needed, for physical and mental health specialists, for tutors in any skill the child wants to learn, for the best possible programs among a variety available to children and youth in any community.

Keniston suggests that the new role for parents is "The Weakened Executive." He points out the "demanding new role" for parents is "choosing, meeting, talking with, and coordinating the experts, the technology, and the institutions that help bring up their children."[8] He points out that in some ways a parent is like the executive in a large firm in that the parent is responsible for the "coordination of the many people and processes that must work together to produce the final product," in this case the healthy, effective adolescent-young adult.

However, he adds, "the parent labors under enormous restrictions." Unlike the executive who "has firm authority and power to influence . . . the decisions of those" with whom he works, "today's parents have little authority over those . . . with whom they share the task of raising their children." Instead, "most parents deal . . . from a position of inferiority" to those with whom they must coordinate. They may feel helpless in dealing with them. "Teachers, doctors, social workers, or television producers possess more status than most parents."[9]

> As a result, the parent today is usually a coordinator without voice or authority, a maestro trying to conduct an orchestra of players who have never met and who play from a multitude of different scores, each in a notation the conductor cannot read. If parents are frustrated, it is no wonder, for although they have the responsibility for their children's lives, they hardly ever have the voice, the authority, or the power to make others listen to them.[10]

Space does not allow me to tell more. I but mention two other factors that can intensify an existing generation gap. One, economic pressures increase father's work hours and cause mother to seek work. This decreases even further any interaction time between parent and adolescent. Two, persons born before or during World War II spent part of their lifetime in the pre-television, pre-nuclear, pre-space technology, pre-computer era. Therefore, they are apt to have a quite different perception of the world today than their offspring who are growing up with all these things. Indeed, in these matters, the young may be more at home, and more wise than their parents. Margaret Mead develops this point in her book *Culture and Commitment.*[11]

A Mid-Life Parental Style

As a middle-age parent, I cannot solve all these issues without difficulty. However, I can develop an appropriate style of parenting that fits who I am, who my adolescent children are, and what the needs of this age are. I offer my conclusions to you as a stimulus to your developing your appropriate style of parenting.

I will be who I am, nothing more, nothing less, neither older, nor younger than I really am. Since I am patient with other people's problems, I will be as patient with those of persons in my family. While I don't reveal all of myself to anyone, as best I can, I will be the same person publicly, in my family life, and in my interior life.

I will make time to share talks and life experiences with my adolescent children. They are just as important as anyone else, and they will be leaving so soon.

I will also try to find some common interests that provide some bonding and shared experiences with my adolescent children. For one of mine the bond is trips and talks; with another bike hikes and tennis; for another photography and basketball.

Rather than bemoan how many forces draw my children and me apart, I will fully celebrate those experiences we deeply share.

I will follow a consistent practice of faith, worship, and service to my church. I will draw them into it but grant a measure of freedom to them to choose for themselves.

I will live out my goals and dreams through me. And I will let them live their dreams and goals through them. I will not lay on them my frustrated ambitions. I had my chance and will let them have theirs.

I will not give them everything they want. But I will give them every opportunity that I can to learn, discover, master a new skill, or develop a new interest. I will try to let nothing stand in the way of their becoming all they want to be.

I will listen a lot. That way I have a better chance of discovering the changing perceptions of my adolescent child. Then, too, people learn by talking and hearing how they sound. I will try not to jump in too quickly with my authoritative views on the subject, nor expect those opinions to be considered the last word.

Since I won't win any popularity contests anyhow, I will make decisions as a parent from my reasoned, open-minded judgment, not what seems easiest or most pleasant at the moment.

I will let go slowly. I know how to say "no" and will say it when I need to. But I aspire to a wisdom that knows when to give more freedom and responsibility. And as they approach their adult years, I will let go, as completely as I can. There will be no apron strings (or whatever a father's counterpart to that is), no emotional blackmail. The only bonds will be those freely chosen out of our love for each other.

I will not let my adolescent children destroy my confidence in myself as a person or a parent. Even if my children find themselves in tragic circumstances and/or totally turned off to me, I will maintain my own sense of worth and dignity. This will be difficult, because they may well tell me loudly and clearly that I was unfair and failed them. Too frequently counselors, court officers, and social workers seem to agree that behind every messed-up teenager, there are parents who failed. From my own experience in counseling, I suspect that frequently teenagers get into difficulty because they made some bad choices, blew some good opportunities, and slapped away the arms outstretched to them! Nor is that adolescent scrape the end of the story! It may be a learning experience on the way to maturity.

I will seek out other parents of adolescents for discussion and support. There are indications that the greatest adult educational need today is in marriage and parenting. Quite possibly, being parents of adolescents is the most sensitive period of the whole parenting process. And so, whether formally or informally, I will reach out. I will give and receive emotional support, benefit from shared experience, and share collective wisdom. This note[12] will refer you to some resources for parents' support groups in addition to the ones already cited in this chapter.

The Mid-Life Child

All of us who are fortunate enough to have our parents while we are in the middle years will probably experience some changes in our relationship with those parents. Again Erma Bombeck will describe her experience for us, and then we shall reflect on ours.

"When Did I Become the Mother and the Mother Become the Child?"

A nuclear physicist once figured out if a woman has a baby when she is twenty years old, she is twenty times as old as the baby.

When the baby is twenty years of age and the mother is forty, she is only twice as old as the child. When the baby is sixty and the mother is eighty, she is only 1 1/3 times as old as the child. When the child is eighty and the mother is one hundred, she is only 1 ¼ times as old as the offspring.

When will the baby catch up with the mother?

When indeed.

Does it begin one night when you are asleep and your mother is having a restless night and you go into her room and tuck her blanket around her bare arms?

Does it appear one afternoon when, in a moment of irritation, you snap, "How can I give you a home permanent if you won't sit still? If you don't care how you look, I do!" (My God, is that an echo?)

Or did it come the rainy afternoon when you were driving home from the store and you slammed on your brakes and your arms sprang protectively between her and the windshield and your eyes met with a knowing, sad look?

The transition comes slowly, as it began between her and her mother. The changing of power. The transferring of responsibility. The passing down of duty. Suddenly you are spewing out the familiar phrases learned at the knee of your mother.

"Of course you're sick. Don't you think I know when you're not feeling well? I'll be over to pick you up and take you to the doctor around eleven. And be ready!"

"So, where's your sweater? You know how cold the stores get with the air conditioning. That's the last thing you need is a cold."
. . .

But slowly and insidiously and certainly the years give way and there is no one to turn to.

"Where are my glasses? I never can find them. Did I fall asleep in the movie again? What was it all about?"

"Dial that number for me. You know how I always get the wrong one."

"I'm not having a Christmas tree this year. There's no one to see it and it just dirties up the carpet for eight months or so."

"Look what I made in macrame today. I'll make you a sling in blue for your kitchen if you want." (It is reminiscent of the small hand in plaster of paris framed over the sofa.) . . .

The daughter isn't ready yet to carry the burden. But the course is set.

The first year you celebrate Thanksgiving at your house and you roast the turkey and your mother sets the table.

The first time you subconsciously turn to her in a movie and say, "Shhhh!"

The first time you rush to grab her arm when she walks over a patch of ice.

As your own children grow strong and independent, the mother becomes more childlike. . . .

The daughter contemplates, "It wasn't supposed to be this way. All the years I was bathed, dressed, fed, advised, disciplined, ordered, cared for, and had every need anticipated, I wanted my turn to come when I could command. Now that it's here, why am I so sad?"

You bathe and pat dry the body that once housed you. You spoon feed the lips that kissed your cuts and bruises and made them well. You comb the hair that used to playfully cascade over you to make you laugh. You arrange the covers over the legs that once carried you high into the air to Banbury Cross.

The naps are frequent as yours used to be. You accompany her to the bathroom and wait to return her to bed. She has a sitter already for New Year's Eve. You never thought it would be like this.

While riding with your daughter one day, she slams on her brakes and her arm flies out instinctively in front of you between the windshield and your body.

My God! So soon.[13]

Our parents are twenty to thirty years older than we. And so they are moving into a "high risk" time of life.

Retirement

greater susceptibility to certain illnesses

reduced physical powers

possible loss of the ability to live independently,
 the loss of a spouse through death,
  the accompanying bereavement and adjustment
—these and more are the "risks" of being old. As one spunky, elderly
man with frail health told me, "Growing old is not for sissies!"

The needs of our elderly parents may cause "role reversal." The
child becomes the parent and the parent becomes the child.

And yet, we may be overreaching if we completely take over our
parents' lives. They may feel quite capable of making decisions and
feel robbed of vital dignity if this is taken away.

Then, too, many factors may stand in the way of your being as
helpful to your aged parents in need as you would like to be. Quite
compact living quarters may mean it is impossible to invite your
parents to move in with you. The needs of spouse and teenage
children may make it impossible to invest a major amount of your
time on your parents' needs. Your own career and community
commitments may have already claimed most of your time and
energy. BUT, your parents need you.

What often follows for the middle-aged child is a feeling of loss and
of guilt. There is the loss of that strong parent on whom you depended
for strength and for wisdom. There is guilt that you are unable to give
as unreservedly to your parents as they gave to you.

A woman in her thirties described it thus—

> "What's happened to me? I'm like the rope in a tug of war between my
> parents and my children. I always seem to be needed in two places at the
> same time and I'm never in the right one. . . . It's awful to feel so guilty all
> the time. But do you know there's something even worse? It's that little
> voice inside my head that's always crying out, 'What about me? When is
> there going to be time for me? Doesn't anybody care?'" [14]

Again, this is overstated. Some of our parents age with remarkably
few illnesses or complaints. They live with vigor and hope to the day
they die. However, the more frequent pattern is probably to have
some stress and strain about parents during our middle years. How
then do I cope?

First, I resolve to be responsible but not a martyr. I do what I can
but do not abandon all that I hold dear for any one responsibility.

Second, I work with all who are concerned. My aged parent, my
brothers and sisters, my spouse and children, community agencies,
and the medical profession can all be drawn into shared responsi-

bility. I cannot and will not solve these issues alone.

Third, I avoid the guilt trip as much as possible. It does not do me or anyone else any good. And we need all the clear insight we can muster. In this period of life I am stretched tight enough that I cannot possibly do all that I should. Accepting that, I let go of most of my guilt about undone tasks.

Fourth, I keep talking with my parents and my family so that we do not withdraw into separate angry shells.

Fifth, I claim peace in the knowledge that God and only God is the One who neither slumbers nor sleeps. I divide my life and time before God with the greatest wisdom I can muster. During such times I just have to leave some things to providence!

Sixth, I claim the opportunity of this experience to be a free mature adult, perhaps for the first time. All my life, I have had a half-hidden dependence on my parents and a need for their approval. Now I can and must decide for myself. I answer to myself and my God for the consequences of my decisions.

The Gospel and My Family Memberships

Basically we dealt with the gospel's perspective in the previous chapter when we noted that human relationships can be the means of divine grace.

But it can be briefly added that the family is especially endowed with grace-full possibilities. The Bible uses both "father" and "mother" as metaphors for God's faithful care of us, love for us, and forgiveness of us. "Brother" and "sister" are terms used to communicate the vital new closeness between Christians. And one image of salvation is that of being adopted into the family of God with Christ as our older brother. The Bible uses these word symbols because the experienced gospel may already be present in family relationships. Though we have been hurt in families, we can also be healed!

9
SHIFTING INTO GROWTH
The Inward Journey

When I first read *Shifting Gears* by Nena and George O'Neill,[1] I experienced a shock of recognition. These authors were clearly stating something I had long felt but had been unable to put into words.

They began by attacking the "maturity myth," which states that if you make the "right choices" in your twenties and thirties, you will be guaranteed fulfillment for the rest of your life. The maturity myth holds promise for five things: that you will be home free; that you "will become less restless and more stable"; that you "will attain emotional security"; that "your sex life will be safe"; and finally, that "the future will be manageable."[2]

Though those promises at first seem attractive, there is a dark side to each of them. The O'Neills' chart shows it this way:[3]

"THE MATURITY MYTH"

"Positive Promises"	*"Negative Corollaries"*
"1. You will be home safe . . . in your forties.	1. Few or no new directions in your life.
"2. You will be less restless and more stable.	2. Less . curiosity about the world, more repetitiveness.

"3. You will have emotional security.

"4. Your sex life will be safe.

"5. Your future will be manageable."

3. Change, whether inner or outer, will be threatening.

4. Waning interest in sex.

5. Future without real challenge.

Instead of the "maturity myth," they subscribe to the process of *open maturity*.[4] They approvingly quote a woman of forty-two who stated:

> If you define maturity as being fully developed, as a peak that you reach and then drop off from, then thank God I will never be mature in that sense. Maturity for me is learning how to develop and *use* all my capacities—it's not reaching any particular goal. Lord knows, I've had plenty of them, and they change and they will continue to change. Maturity for me is process, the process of becoming more of myself and continually growing.[5]

The O'Neills are holding before us the concept of "Creative Maturity." They see maturity not as a firm, static destination. Rather, they see it as a process of becoming. In other words, mature equals maturing. Their concept of maturity offers an important perspective to us middle-agers as we consider the possibilities of personal growth.

I am convinced that not only do we go through developmental crises and tasks in the mid-years, but we also face opportunities for dynamic growth and becoming that can make our adjustment to these years better or worse.

Therefore, I am going to suggest briefly five possible growth areas to you. (The last two areas are discussed in chapter 10.) Of course, you may choose to grow in quite different directions. At any rate, here are some possibilities for both inner and outer growth.

I Choose to Grow Spiritually

"I'm convinced that man's search at midlife is ultimately a spiritual one."[6]

"Among all my patients in the second half of life—that is to say, over 35—there has not been one whose problem in the last resort was not that of finding a religious outlook on life."[7]

". . . I am given to understand that some Eastern Traditions will not admit a man to a school of meditation until he is forty."[8]

These three statements suggest something very striking about us mid-lifers: (*a*) a secular writer suggests our mid-life *dilemma* is ultimately spiritual; (*b*) a noted psychiatrist tells us the *solution* to our dilemma is essentially spiritual; and (*c*) some eastern traditions have discovered that those over forty possibly have a special spiritual *aptitude!*

Taken together, these statements suggest an urgency about spiritual growth in the mid-years and the opportunity for exciting spiritual development that we may not have imagined possible.

If we hunger for dynamic, spiritual becoming, how do we go about obtaining it? A discovery about the direction of our orientation as mid-lifers suggest the direction this spiritual development might take. This discovery is the growing "evidence which indicates that, beginning in the forties, there appear in [persons] the . . . signs of a major redirection from *outer* to *inner* concerns." There is the need to reorient one's life from an inner perspective. Not all of us heed this need, and, therefore,

> there are sad examples of failures in this area—empty, driving, hollow persons whose life-ambitions are pitifully inadequate when measured against the possibilities of the human spirit. And there are beautiful successes—persons moving steadily into another intensity, a deeper communion.[9]

Spiritual growth for mid-life must not be "growth in general." Rather, it must be connected to the person's inner needs, the person's life story, the person's life issues.

It seems most likely that spiritual growth for the mid-life person will be relational. It is growth that can best take place by finding or creating a group of people who are in the midst of their mid-life years and who have the possibility of developing some trust and support among them. Below I would like to suggest some exercises a group of mid-life persons could participate in to aid spiritual growth.

First, I suggest you get in touch with inner needs. To do so, you might engage in this growth exercise that Howard Clinebell suggests. His original plan is that one do this with one's spouse (and that may be the mid-life trust group you form, just you and her, or you and him). However, it is equally useful if you use it in a group a bit larger. Take turns completing the following questions. After all have shared, take as much time as you need to discuss the issues and feelings that arise.

"The ideas and issues which excite me most are . . . ;" "The things that are most worth living for right now are . . . ;" "I feel the most joy (pain, hope, lonely, together) when . . . ;" "What I really believe about God is . . . ;" "I feel closest to (most distant from) God when . . . ;" "I get spiritually high when . . . ;" "The beliefs that mean the most to me now are . . . ;" "The beliefs from my childhood which no longer make sense are . . . ;" "Life has the least (the most) meaning for me when . . . ;" "I feel closest to you (most distant from you) spiritually when . . . ;" "The way I really feel about the church is . . . ;" "I'd like to do the following, to enjoy more spiritual sharing . . . ;" "To enrich the spiritual life of our family, I'd like to . . . ;" "Other things about our spiritual growth that concern me are . . . ;" "The way I feel about discussing these questions is. . . ."[10]

Such an experience can help one become more aware of spiritual resources and needs within as well as those of others.

Second, I suggest you examine your life story and the spiritual pilgrimage that is part of that story. Up until recently, the years from thirty to sixty were viewed as a static, unexciting time, a plateau of nongrowth and nondevelopment. Even with the recent discovery of adult development life stages, we still do not have many structures for telling and examining our life stories together. As one woman put it, "If you are productive and not disrupting the external order, no one cares what is going on inside." Worse yet, as a woman friend pointed out to me, if a woman is not productive, too often no one even notices her or is concerned about her.

To focus on your inner journey through adult years will probably be a new experience for you personally and for your church. But rich spiritual enrichment awaits the effort. Henry C. Simmons suggests that our programs of religious education should create opportunities

"Every one of us has a public duty to answer these questions:
1. What do you plan to do with the rest of your life?
2. What do you want your neighborhood to be like in the next five years? Who will take responsibility for changing/conserving it?
3. Who should plan the future? What work must be done to guarantee the future?
4. What new processes and institutions are needed for human goals? for the well-being of the people?
I believe we stand precariously on the brink—we have the capacity to destroy our society or to heal and humanize it."

Maggie Kuhn, *Maggie Kuhn on Aging,* edited by Dieter Hessel (Philadelphia: The Westminster Press, 1977), p. 125.

for allowing middle-agers to tell and share their stories. Further, the leadership should help the storyteller focus on the inner life, not simply marker events.[11]

Simmons has been experimenting with this examination of the inner journey in adult Christian education programs. He writes:

> During the past few years I have had the opportunity to ask many adults to share with me the story of the development of their faith. The first reaction is standard: "Sure, but I don't really have anything great to say. You'll have to ask me a lot of questions." One and a half or two hours later I have asked very few questions; and I am deeply moved by the intensity and drama of the story of the inner journey. Most have never told the story to anyone before.[12]

Explore your story. Discover the spiritual dimension within it. Claim that story as yours. There is a spiritual power in doing so.

Third, discover the spiritual interaction with your life issues. In this book, at the end of each chapter that explores a life issue, I have offered a section on the perspective of biblical faith. In those same groups you have now formed, you may want to go on to talk about these life issues in interaction with your faith. Those sections of this book might provide you some kernels with which to start. But ultimately you will need to ask more directly: What is my problem, and how do my spiritual resources and faith perspective help me grapple with it?

Fourth, let your self-discoveries lead you on to vigorous study and exploration. Perhaps you found that you need a deeper understanding of Bible, church history, theology, Christian ethics or personality and religion. Possibly you discovered a hunger to engage more completely in some of the disciplines and resources of the faith, such as prayer, meditation, worship, journalizing, and witness.

In understanding the spiritual growth available to us in mid-life, I am helped by John H. Westerhoff's concept of four different types of faith (a) "Experienced faith"—the experiences of trust, love, and acceptance so important to a life of faith—usually occur in *childhood* (though not exclusively there). (b) "Affiliative faith"—the sense of belonging, of having affections for one's faith, and a sense of authority about it—may well occur in *youth*. (c) "Searching faith"— the action of doubt, of critical judgment, of experimentation, of discovering the need to commit—may occur in *young adult years*. (d) "Owned faith"—a sense of grasping the realities that have grasped us—is shown in ability to witness in word and deed. One experiences a unity of personal identity as a person of faith. A person discovers that this committed stance is God's intention for every person, approximates one's full potential, and experiences deep meaning and purpose in this discovery. This occurs in *adult years.*

Westerhoff suggests that this lifetime movement from experienced faith through affiliative and searching faith to owned faith is *conversion;* conversion is more typically a process by which persons are nurtured in a community of faith (the religion of the heart), go through the despair of doubt and the intellectual quest for understanding (the religion of the head), and at last experience illumination, certainty, and identity.[13] Fellow middle-agers, our conversion continues! More vistas of spiritual becoming call us.

I Choose to Grow in Intimacy and Relationships

If I told you two people were intimate, what would you think? I thought so! It just goes to show how we've abused that word "intimacy" in our culture. Two people can have sex without being intimate, and two people can be intimate without having sex!

Our society neither understands nor encourages truly intimate relationships, and all of us are the poorer. One of the saddest discoveries Levinson made in his depth study of forty men had to do with friendship.

> . . . we would say that close friendship with a man or woman is rarely experienced by American men. . . . most men do not have an intimate male friend of the kind that they recall fondly from boyhood or youth. Many men have had casual dating relationships with women, and perhaps a few complex love-sex relationships, but most men have not had an intimate non-sexual friendship with a woman. We need to understand why friendship is so rare and what consequences this deprivation has for adult life.[14]

The more I observe life, the more I am convinced of the accuracy of Levinson's observation. Many men do not often form deep trusting friendships with men, nor do all women form deep trusting friendships with women. And frequently spouses discourage their partners from friendships with persons of the opposite sex. We hope for intimacy with our spouses, but too seldom do we work at and achieve that goal.

We hesitate to move toward intimacy partly out of distrust and partly out of competitiveness. Then, too, our situation is complicated by our highly mobile situation. This mobility causes separation from old friends and can make us wonder whether it is worth the effort and the time invested to start over again.

BUT, our children are flying the nest. Mid-life is filled with unique pains and special joys. Sorrow is diminished and joy is enhanced if shared with good friends.

I am convinced that one's spouse should be the first one in the circle of intimacy for married people. For many, this will take some new skills and effort. However, he or she should not be the only one. For one thing, we live in a much too uncertain world. What if that spouse dies or leaves you? You would discover that you built your support base too narrow. Further, certainly no one's world is so small that his or her spouse is the only trustworthy person.

If you agree on this need for intimacy and relationships, how do you start in developing them? You begin by finding that person or group that holds the promise of being able to form a trustful, mutual, growth relationship with you. This could be a group formed to discuss mid-life issues such as we just discussed. (That is the formal way you start. How much more fortunate if an acquaintanceship grows to the point where you sense these qualities are becoming part of your relationship.) You propose to that person(s) a covenanted relationship where there is respect for identity, equality, and integrity of the other. You make very explicit promises about the honesty of self-disclosure with each other and the keeping of each other's self-disclosures in strictest confidence.

The O'Neills again help us at this point: "Intimacy is listening to another person's disclosures and caring about their meaning to the other person's growth. Intimacy is also caring enough to disclose yourself to others—making the effort and taking the risk involved in opening yourself up to another."[15] Out of this comes emotional closeness, encouragement of mutual growth and self-discovery.

Howard Clinebell told of a person longing for a relationship so intimate that "just once in my life, we could touch souls."[16] Perhaps as you examine your life, you will center upon just the same need. If so, give it a focused priority.

I Will Grow in My Ability to Deal with My Aging, Retirement, and Death

The other day two early mid-life women were talking together in our church office, bemoaning the coming years and what the years would do to their appearance. They are both attractive persons, and with a combination of truthfulness and chivalry, I told them they need not worry. I assured them they would still be attractive for many years to come; after all, I was older than they. But one of them responded, "That's different. Older men are distinguished! But older women are wrinkly—and fading."

If that is a cliché, it is an all too deeply engrained one in our society. How unfair we are! In the popular myth of our culture, a man can be considered attractive at any age. But if a woman is to be attractive, she needs to be eighteen—"Miss America"—or hide the fact she is not.

One of my most pleasant discoveries on my thirtieth birthday was how really beautiful thirty-year-old women are! And one of the happiest discoveries of my fortieth birthday was that beauty, fascination, charm—in either sex—is not age related at all. Our culture has misled us into thinking that, for women at least, beauty is found only in one stage of life rather than in all of life.

If we admit that our society is wrong about the relationship of beauty and age, what understanding do we put in its place? We might begin with the basic view that aging is built into the very fabric of life. Aging is part of living. It is not something that occurs at a given time in life; it occurs in all of life.

Dr. Nathan W. Shock reports, "The first general finding in gerontology is that the body dies a little every day."[17] Researchers have discovered that aging is a gentle process that begins about the thirtieth birthday. Human abilities do not suddenly decline at sixty-five or any other age. Rather, the output of the heart and the speed of nerve impulses decline gradually—at about the same rate from sixty to seventy as they did between thirty and forty. (And we all know that we are highly vigorous, capable people at forty, don't we?) The aging person (of any age) faces two possibilities: "He may mature and grow in grace and power of relationship; or he may deteriorate and dehumanize."[18] The choice of growth and maturity often causes the accompanying aging to slow down even to the very end.

In her collection of poems about middle-age, Judith Viorst writes one about the question of middle age: Should I be realizing my potential or accepting my limitations? Those most hopeful observers of the aging answer, "You should be doing both." Accept those limitations that aging brings, but be open to ever new potential.

If we are struggling with the agony of anticipation of mid-life aches and pains, we need not see that as a sign of inevitable decline. We can be reminded that people have demonstrated continued growth and competence into their advanced years. At Age seventy-seven, Golda Meir was asked to rejuvenate Israel's Labor party. George Burns was eighty when he made his film comeback in *The Sunshine Boys* and won his first Oscar. When he was eighty-nine, Artur Rubinstein played "better than ever" in a Carnegie Hall recital. And the elderly Florida Scott-Maxwell informs us:

> Age puzzles me. I thought it was a quiet time. My seventies were interesting, and fairly serene, but my eighties are passionate. I grow more intense as I age. To my own surprise I burst out with hot conviction.[19]

Bernice Neugarten has suggested that a new term is needed to describe those elderly persons who are retired but who are healthy, vigorous, educated, and still learning, capable of community or political involvement. Such persons may have time on their hands that can be used for self-enhancement or community participation. Neugarten has termed such people the *"young old,"* a term that has gained wider acceptance than most of the usual phrases used to describe these vigorous elderly persons.[20]

Countless examples reinforce the truth that we can choose growth and choose usefulness and, hence, deal with our aging in a grace-filled manner. I cannot avoid aging, but, until my body wears out, I can elect to be "young old."

However, somewhere along the line in this aging process, there comes an event which, unless properly anticipated and prepared for, can be a real blow to growing old gracefully. I refer to retirement, which may be the biggest difficulty in our resolve to deal creatively with aging. In that connection we will do well to consider David Ray's "Ten Rules for Retirement Preparation." Here are his suggestions.

1. "Begin Planning Your Retirement . . . Now!" He suggests one start planning retirement twenty years in advance. It should be planned on the "installment plan" so that as well as possible one has planned for health, economic satisfaction, and happiness for oneself and one's partner.

2. "Make Your Life Meaningful." Carry on your search for meaning now among those resources you will still have available when you retire.

3. "Accept the Process of Getting Older." Enough said?

4. "Think Ahead Financially." Have some investment plan and understanding of what your financial experience will be in retirement.

5. "Start Now to Grow the Habit of Showing Happiness."

6. "Step by Step, Change from Making a Living to Making a Life." Discover that you are first a person and, second, a worker.

7. "Shape Up." Your body is the baggage you carry on the pilgrimage through life. The more excess baggage one carries, the shorter the trip.

8. "Develop the Positive Power Within You."

9. "Maintain a Hopeful Outlook on Life."

10. "Start Letting Others Help You." Move into interdependence.[21]

According to Ray, men need to start planning their retirement in their forties, using the considerations he has just mentioned. However, Virginia Pipe has pointed out that "retirement planning" may be experienced quite differently by women:

> Women whose career has been motherhood need to plan their retirement at the birth of their last child. They, like professional athletes, have a forced early retirement after fifteen to twenty years at their career. A second career, a retirement career, if you will, needs to be planned because of the forced retirement for the first career.[22]

What I hear Virginia telling us is that for many women, retirement does not come neatly toward the end of life. Rather, it occurs in young adult years, in the middle, and near the end!

Eventually, at some point in my aging (either before my retirement or after), I will die. How strange that sounds to the ear—"I will die." From the general acknowledgment of that fact and the ordering of life in the light of it, I can grow in a depth appreciation of that fact. Then I can take steps to plan that my death expresses the meaning of my life and makes it easier for my survivors. As I grow in my ability to deal with my death, I am able to make the following decisions.

1. I go to an attorney and prepare a will. This will, in addition to including provisions for my family survivors, includes symbolic statements and contributions to those causes in which I deeply believe. My will is going to be carefully read some day by those I most want to influence after I am gone. It ought to be a reminder of who I am and what I believe.

2. Within my will, or beyond it, I make provision that some of those special objects I own be given to the person for whom they would hold most meaning. In my case, some of those objects would be my extensive library on ministry, my musical instruments, and my camera. What do you own that you would most want some particular person to have?

3. I anticipate and deal with some of the issues that may surround my dying. This paragraph from the "Living Will" says it rather well:

> If the situation should arise in which there is no reasonable expectation of my recovery from physical or mental disability, I request that I be allowed to die and not be kept alive by artificial means or "heroic measures." I do not fear death itself as much as the indignities of deterioration, dependence, and hopeless pain. I, therefore, ask that the medication be mercifully administered to me to alleviate suffering even though this may hasten the moment of death.[23]

4. I make plans for my funeral or memorial service that will express my faith and life. Copies should be given to my pastor and (since I will probably have another pastor before I need him for this purpose) with the person in my family who will most understand.

5. I make plans for any organ donations, medical use of my body, disposal of my body, grave plot, funeral director, and burial. Most funeral homes are open to people who wish to speak with them or give instructions in writing. (If you need help with these sorts of decisions, the Funeral and Memorial Society can give you informed counsel. For the address of the society nearest you, contact: Continental Association of Funeral and Memorial Societies, Inc., 1828 L Street, NW, Washington, DC 20036.

Having made these decisions, one does not need to rush to implement them! However, from many years as a pastor, I can tell you, mourning and surviving a loved one has been least difficult when the one who died frankly faced his or her mortality and had faced and resolved such issues. After you have made those decisions, be on with the task of claiming the years you have for a very special kind of growing.

10

SHIFTING INTO GROWTH
(continued)

The Outward Journey

I Choose to Grow Morally—Ethically

Recently some of us parents heard a disturbing rumor. We heard that the exciting, experimental open-classroom public school that our children attended was going to be reviewed. We immediately became concerned that the school board might terminate this experimental school that had been so helpful to our children.

So we banded together, surveyed other parents, and put our information together into a convincing (we hoped) presentation.

I was asked to serve as spokesperson for our group. We appeared before the proper committee of the school board. I gave it all that I had, and we fielded the questions. When we finished, they agreed we had put on a good show and concurred that our school should stay open for some time longer.

We parents walked out with the warm glow of a citizens' action group that has succeeded. And so, we bade each other good-night and went our separate ways.

On the way home, the thought hit me, "What was I so excited about? My youngest daughter finishes with that school in two months! My family will never need it again." Once that rather selfish thought floated through my head, the broader issue came to mind,

"Will I continue to be concerned about public education when my children have completed it? Will I be as concerned over other child issues and organizations as I now am?"

My experience represents one mid-life temptation to begin to have a shrinking moral-ethical concern. We discover that activities which had seemed public spirited we really did to provide for our own children.

But we can experience another temptation to accept moral-ethical shrinkage. This temptation comes from the understanding of ourselves as developing, changing persons. And therefore there may be an overemphasis on "me." In a penetrating critique of Levinson's *Seasons of a Man's Life* (a volume to which we have referred frequently), James Sloan Allen detects that the book contains not only a psychology but also a morality of development. Allen charges that Levinson canonizes (or makes sacred) "personal development." He cites Levinson's statement, "The developing individual is like a long-distance traveler: from time to time he changes vehicles, fellow passengers and baggage of all kinds." This seems to speak of no lasting commitment, no enduring responsibility to persons, to values, to anything. The only rule is "personal growth" to the exclusion of other loyalties. The persons who absolutize personal growth then "shrink from lasting obligations and difficult sacrifices, turning instead toward their private needs, whose demands . . . are sovereign."[1]

To summarize Allen's concern, it is that "I, me, my, and my personal growth" become a person's sole concern to the exclusion of "costly relationships, sacrificial caring, lasting commitments." Indeed, much popular psychology of our decade smacks of this emphasis. The 1970s have been called the "Me" decade. Tom Wolfe in a penetrating analysis of this movement notes how widespread this view is throughout our entire culture. In this article he recalls a copy-writer named Shirley Polykoff who (while working on the Clairol hair-dye account) came up with the line: "If I've only one life, let me live it as a blonde." In a single slogan, she quite unintentionally summed up the theme of the "Me" decade. "If I've only one life, let me live it as a _____!" (Fill in the blank as you please.)[2] This was not only a secular movement, in Wolfe's opinion. It became elevated to a religious movement—so intense that he terms it the "Third Great Awakening."

There is a tragic aspect of the "Me" decade. When one lives by the slogan "If I've only one life, let me live it as a _____," one is cut off from one of the most basic assumptions of society—humankind's age-old belief in serial immortality, that is, that somehow each of us lives our life not merely for ourselves, but for those generations that come before and after—of whom we are a part.

> The husband and wife who sacrifice their own ambitions and their material assets in order to provide a "better future" for their children . . . the soldier who risks his life . . . in battle . . . the man who devotes his life to some struggle for "his people" that cannot possibly be won in his lifetime . . . and, for that matter, most women upon becoming pregnant for the first time . . . are people who conceive of themselves . . . as part of a great biological stream. Just as something of their ancestors lives on in them, so will something of them live on in their children . . . or in their people, their race, their community. . . .[3]

Levinson is not unmindful of this issue. He writes, "A major developmental task of middle adulthood is *to find a better balance between the needs of the self and the needs of society.*"[4] But the critic who finds Levinson weighting the personal development heavier than the needs of society is quite probably right.

Well, then, we have at least two temptations to have a smaller-than-life moral ethical view. The two temptations are *(a)* the mid-lifer's developing "empty nest" may lure one to shed many causes that she or he supported simply for the sake of the children; *(b)* self-growth psychology, while lending rich insight for development in some areas, may influence persons to emphasize growth at the cost of all other commitments.

And yet, we are persons whose experience can help us develop a much broader perspective. This is a perspective our communities, nation, and world very much need. However, if we are going to offer that much needed perspective, we will need to let our moral-ethical life be one of our growing edges.

There may be a clue for us about our moral development in Lawrence Kohlberg's concept of the Six Moral Stages of Development. These are as follows:

Stage 1. "Heteronomous Morality"—One wishes to avoid punishment so discerns the superior power of authorities. "I do what I am told or I will be punished."

Stage 2. "Individualism"—One follows rules because it is to one's best interest, and wants to be fair in letting others do the same.

Stage 3. "Mutual Interpersonal Expectations, Conformity"—One lives up to what the significant people in his or her life expect of him or her in such roles as friend, brother or sister, son or daughter, etc.

Stage 4. "Social System and Conscience"—One upholds laws of society except in extreme cases when they are in conflict with other social duties. One is committed to the whole social institution and to fulfilling agreed upon duties.

Stage 5. "Social Contract or Utility and Individual Rights"—A person has a sense of obligation to obey law because it contributes to the welfare of all and the protection of all people's rights.

Stage 6. "Universal Ethical Principles"—One has self-chosen ethical principles. One usually chooses to obey laws or social agreements because they rest on such principles. When laws violate these principles, however, one acts in accordance with the principles. These principles will include justice, equality of human rights, and respect for the dignity of human beings.[5]

Some critics suggest there is another stage of moral development beyond Kohlberg's sixth—namely, the stage of altruistic, selfless, outgoing love.

What Is Success?

To laugh often and love much;
To win the respect of intelligent persons and the affection of children;
To earn the approval of honest critics and endure the betrayal of false friends;
To appreciate beauty;
To find the best in others;
To give of one's self without the slightest thought of return;
To have accomplished a task, whether by a healthy child, a rescued soul, a garden patch or a redeemed social condition;
To have played and laughed with enthusiasm and sung with exaltation;
To know that even one life has breathed easier because you have lived;
This is to have succeeded.   —Anonymous

Richard Bolles, *The Three Boxes of Life* (Berkeley, Calif.: Ten Speed Press, 1978), p. 325. Used by special permission. Those desiring a copy of the complete book for further reading may procure it from the publisher, Ten Speed Press, P.O. Box 7123, Berkeley, CA 94707.

But let's return to our discussion of our moral, ethical growth. Kohlberg points out that the first two of these stages is the level of most children under age nine, some adolescents, and many criminal offenders. We find most adolescents and adults in our society in stages three and four. Stages five and six are reached only by a small minority of adults, and usually reached only after the age of twenty.[6]

Take a look at those stages and ask yourself some questions. At what stage am I? Where would I like to be? Do I consistently stay at one stage or do I move back and forth between stages? Do I think on one stage and act on another? Would I be able to remain at the stage where I am if my economic well-being was threatened? If my physical well-being was threatened? Can I write out in a paragraph or two the moral-ethical stance on which I build my life?

As you attempt to write that brief statement of your moral-ethical stance, consider: How ought I choose? What should I choose? For whose sake should I choose? In what social context shall I choose?

Think about some of the most difficult decisions you have ever faced. How do you decide when neither side is all "black" or "white" but both are shades of gray? How do you decide when you will not be happy with either decision? How do you decide when someone will be hurt regardless of what you decide?

When some persons face such difficult decisions at work, they sometimes conclude that they have to leave their religious faith in the parking lot of their place of work. They feel that there's no place for faith in such rough-and-tumble decisions.

If you have thought that, I urge you to reconsider. The God who loves and justifies us freely out of grace accepts us in our place of vagueness and ambiguity. We don't have to be right to be justified and loved by God.

But, on the other hand, we are called to grow ever more thoughtful and perceptive in our difficult deciding. For we decide in the name of the One who affirmed that our responsibility can be distilled down to, "You shall love the Lord your God with all your heart, and with all your soul, and with all your strength, and with all your mind; and your neighbor as yourself" (Luke 10:27).

These are difficult issues with which to wrestle. And yet they are most important. Without a balanced broad moral-ethical vision, the spiritual growth I just described to you can degenerate into another "Me" decade phenomenon. That is to say, spirituality without ethics can become baptized and sanctified selfishness.

But perhaps there is a more manageable way to think about our moral-ethical growth. Perhaps we should view it more concretely. Therefore, let us state it another way.

I Will Grow in My Vision of the World As God Intends It

Quite often as I think of the swirling change I have encountered in my world in my forty-five years of life, I find myself stretched to the breaking point. Sometimes it seems that I've coped until I've run out of cope. Frequently change has been a way of life. Occasionally it seems that responding and reacting to change takes most of my energy.

It is time to take initiative again—in my mind, first of all, and there if not anywhere else—to ask, "What dreams, visions, goals do I have for this world in which I live?" Perhaps it is time for you to revisit those youthful dreams you had. Can you recall the dreams of your youth? Did they have to do mostly with your personal accomplishments? Or did you have altruistic dreams as well? One of my recurring youthful dreams had to do with a uniquely dynamic, creative, and growing church community. (And frankly, I always had a starring role in this dream.) The dreams had their meaning and value. Since middlescence is the reconsidering of many youthful themes, perhaps it's time to dream again. Instead of impatient, naive dreams, we need to look within for "realistic" dreams. From youthful dreams (where we had a starring role), we need to move on to more mature dreams that have value whether we have a role in them or not.

And for Christians, mid-life dreams need to be formulated in depth dialogue with the vision that arises out of faith-perspective. Our faith affirms a God who is actively involved in the world and all its history. In our limitations we are not asked to respond to all needs and cries of history. But we are expected to listen perceptively for those that uniquely speak to us, and we are called to respond.

Where do you hear God calling you from the needs of the world? Where are world problems touching your sensitivity? To what is God calling you? To what world need or world transformation? To what tiny need? Or tiny transformation?

Or to put it another way, what current problem (local, regional, or world) most upsets you? (Say it out loud or write it down.) Write what the solution to the problem might look like. What is the positive good for which you are hoping? And then ask, in what way is God calling you to be a part of that solution?

Let me give a few examples of the way some persons respond to these questions. Recently a group of concerned people who had a growing awareness of the tremendous gap between rich nations and poor nations felt a need to take a step of personal commitment. They wanted their own lives to bear expression of that commitment. And so they wrote what has become known as the Shakertown Pledge.

> Recognizing that the earth and the fulness thereof is a gift from our gracious God, and that we are called to cherish, nurture, and provide loving stewardship for the earth's resources, and recognizing that life itself is a gift, and a call to responsibility, joy and celebration,
> I make the following declarations:
> 1. I declare myself to be a world citizen.
> 2. I commit myself to lead an ecologically sound life.
> 3. I commit myself to lead a life of creative simplicity and to share my personal wealth with the world's poor.
> 4. I commit myself to join with others in the reshaping of institutions in order to bring about a more just global society in which all people have full access to the needed resources for their physical, emotional, intellectual, and spiritual growth.
> 5. I commit myself to occupational accountability, and so doing I will seek to avoid the creation of products which cause harm to others.
> 6. I affirm the gift of my body and commit myself to its proper nourishment and physical well-being.
> 7. I commit myself to examine continually my relations with others, and to attempt to relate honestly, morally, and lovingly to those around me.
> 8. I commit myself to personal renewal through prayer, meditation, and study.
> 9. I commit myself to responsible participation in a community of faith.[7]

That is a way of responding to a vision of a more just world in regard to the distribution of scarce resources.

For others the vision of the world as God wants it may be tied up to that "Dream" of which Martin Luther King, Jr., spoke in front of the Lincoln Monument in 1963. Our active vision and commitment may be to build a more basic justice and a deeper sense of trust and friendship between persons of various ethnic groups.

For others of us the vision may be concerned with the basic rights and needs of the world's children. Others of us may dream of building more loving and endurable marriage and family patterns.

What is your vision of the world as God intends it to be? Will you grow in your movement toward being a part of that vision?

Faith and Growth

Centuries ago a magnificent, maturing Christian had come to his point of greatest compassion and radiant faith. He was in prison, facing trial and impending death.

However, in writing his concept of Christian growth, he ignored both his marvelous progress and his possible sentence of death. Instead he wrote: "Not that I have already obtained this or am already perfect; but I press on to make it my own, because Christ Jesus has made me his own. . . . One thing I do, forgetting what lies behind and straining forward to what lies ahead, I press on toward the goal for the prize of the upward call of God in Christ Jesus" (Philippians 3:12-14).

This is how growing Christians have always felt. And it's strange. So often the persons with the tiniest commitment find themselves bored, listless, without growth objectives. The magnificent, maturing Christian sees all sorts of growth possibilities ahead.

For the Christian, becoming is like walking to the horizon. When you reach that one, there's another one beckoning to you.

11

THE DESTRUCTION THAT WASTES AT NOONDAY

A Theology of Middle Age

"My God, in whom I trust."
  For he will deliver you. . . .
  You will not fear . . .
    . . . the destruction that wastes at noonday.
                    —Psalm 91:2*b,* 3, 5, 6

As we conclude this conversation together, let's explore more explicitly the interaction between the Christian faith and the mid-life dilemma. I want to attempt to develop a beginning theology of middle age. However, perhaps "theology of middle age" is too grandiose a term for this sharing. For I simply want to explore those aspects of the Christian gospel that speak to middle adults with a special poignancy. At the same time, middle adults respond to these aspects of the gospel with an urgency and increased sensitivity. Thus, I suspect, "old" Christian teachings become new again for us. What appears "old hat" to others may for us become an intensely appreciated and integrated faith-style of life. The gospel meets us at the point of our newly discovered personal vulnerability and points to the Power that enables us to cope and triumph.

I once heard one of my theological professors contend, "You never really hear the gospel until you are uprooted." He was thinking largely in sociological-cultural terms and was pointing out that war, depression, the advent of the nuclear era, and other such events uprooted people so that they were shaken out of complacency. In their need, they "heard the gospel"; that is, they sensed their need for it and responded to it. Well, we middle-agers have another source of uprootedness: namely, our creaturely existence, which we have discovered is not just a vague concept "out there" but frighteningly real and personal. Therefore, let us explore those aspects of theology-gospel that speak most directly to us.

First, *a theology of middle age is a theology of providence and finitude.*

In a classic, oft-quoted article, Elliot Jacques spoke of "Death and the Mid-Life Crisis." He suggested, "The paradox is that of entering the prime of life, the stage of fulfillment, but at the same time the prime and fulfillment are dated. Death lies beyond." [1]

Since growing awareness of your own death is a most basic aspect of mid-life, I have attempted to look at that issue unblinkingly with you. My goal is that you and I avoid and deny this subject no longer, but absorb it, and then find the resources for accepting it.

Therefore, a starting point in a theology of middle age is to view this reality of finitude from the perspective of faith. Whatever hope we have for resurrection or immortality, it won't happen in *this* physical body on this planet. We are granted a limited term here.

The theological concept that gives us an overview of this reality is *providence.* Providence is the view that "everything that happens in the universe happens as the result of God's will and in order to accomplish His purpose." [2] This does not mean that the Christian faith claims to have explanations for all events or pat answers to humankind's most perplexing questions. However, the Christian faith "rather proclaims that all events in nature and in history, however bewildering, are ultimately subject to God's purpose." [3]

Therefore, in the providence of God, there is birth, life, and death—including my birth, my life, my death. In providence, God created both birth and death. My faith affirms that God is love and that God creates and provides in love what is best for us, the children of creation. Therefore, my finitude is within the providence of God.

In a lecture on the theology of middle age, Dr. Kenneth Mitchell affirmed, "Our finitude is the evidence of providence. It is God who has given us what we are and who has set the limits to our existence." [4]

A certain inner freedom may come from knowing I am finite within God's providence. For as Herbert Anderson has suggested:

> finitude makes completeness possible. . . . The awareness of finitude is also a gracious moment. All of our achievements are finite but so are our failures. Our lives are finally judged according to limited possibilities. We are free to live and love and learn in the confidence that the God who ordained the boundaries of our life will accept our finite completeness.[5]

One of the "finitude verses" that touches me deeply comes from the Old Testament. King Solomon is dedicating the beautiful temple that he has built. Solomon recalls, "Now it was in the heart of David my father to build a house for the name of the Lord . . ." (2 Chronicles 6:7). However, the Lord counseled David, ". . . you did well that it was in your heart; nevertheless you shall not build the house . . ." (2 Chronicles 6:8-9). As with David, you and I have many more dreams, ideas, and projects than we will ever complete. This verse reminds me that God accepts our finite limitations and reassuringly whispers to each of us, "You did well that it was in your heart." (If you are interested in sticky, theological points, consult this note. If not, go on.)[6]

Second, *a theology of middle age is a theology of pilgrimage.* For those of us who share the Judeo-Christian heritage, the prime example of one on pilgrimage has always been Abraham. He obeyed the call of God to move out from a secure settlement to a life of insecurity. He "went out, not knowing where he was to go . . . sojourned in the land of promise, as in a foreign land, living in tents . . ." (Hebrews 11:8b-9).

Along the pilgrimage of his life, he made many mistakes. He pretended his wife was his sister to protect his own safety. Also, in impatience, he sired a son by the wrong woman.

Abraham also found himself severely tested along the pilgrimage of life; he waited seemingly endless years for the first sign of fulfillment of the hope that he would be the father of a great nation. Then, when that child came, he was asked to make an unspeakable sacrifice.

"For he looked forward to the city which has foundations, whose builder and maker is God" (Hebrews 11:10). (See the original story in Genesis 12–25.) Like Abraham, we live in our pilgrimage in profound insecurity.

Robert Raines writes:

At midlife the certainties of early adulthood fade, are shed, or are torn away. We learn that life gives no guarantees, that there are no earthly absolutes.

In my own midlife journey, I have let go all certainties but one . . . a trusting hope, namely, that nothing can separate me from the love of God come clear in Jesus. . . . I do not have security; I trust. I do not know; I believe.[7]

The image of *pilgrimage* implies two subimages, the *journey* and the *destination*. For this image to inform us, we need to keep both of those subimages in mind and not overemphasize either.

There was a time when to speak of Christian pilgrimage was to emphasize the *destination*—death in this world and life with God in the next. For example, I remember a choir anthem we used to sing when I was a teenager, "Oh, I'm a pilgrim, and I'm a stranger. And I can tarry, I can tarry, but a night." Since that theme made no sense at all to us young people, we engaged in quite irreverent joking and horseplay while the soloist sang the long, sad verses leading up to that refrain. Now, from a later vantage point in life, I see that the song had a point, though it should not be overemphasized. Our pilgrimage is not an aimless wandering. We are moving through life, from God, with God, to God, within God's purposes. There is a destination to which we all travel.

But equally to be emphasized is the *journey*. One Sunday after I had spoken in the morning worship service about faith and the human pilgrimage, a parishioner came up to me and said, "The discoveries about all the dynamic growing for adults may not be *the* good news, but it is certainly good news!" A theology of journey stirs awareness that while there are jars, shocks, surprises, sudden turns, *all* of the journey is to be treasured. (Maybe when we discover this, we won't try to replay that leg of the journey called "youth" over and over again. Maybe society will discover there are some other exciting people around besides young people.) The pilgrim is on a journey of exciting discovery and becoming.

And so faith enables us to perceive that we are on a journey, moving toward a destination which is an appointment with the One who has been our unseen Guide throughout the pilgrimage. Our death awareness makes us conscious of the destination. Our Life Stage development awareness makes us conscious of the adventurous journey.

Third, *a theology of middle age is a theology of managership.*

Managership—that's a word middle-agers should readily understand and to which they can relate! For if there is a characteristic occupation of persons in mid-life, it is managing. We administer the industries, governments, schools, churches, and other institutions of society. (At least middle-age men do. Middle-age women in the most typical career path are winding down managing a household and looking for new responsibilities—opportunities.) Quite possibly the responsibilities of managership weigh heavily enough on our shoulders that we shudder to think of any more responsibilities.

However, the Bible makes clear that this is an image which helps us understand what life is. Actually, we have often missed this central teaching because the Bible's most typical word for manager is "steward." We have perverted the term "stewardship" to mean what we put in the offering plate. In actuality, my gifts, important as they are, constitute only a small part of what it means to be a manager-steward of God's resources.

Jesus put the matter most vividly in Matthew 25:14-30, the parable of the talents. You recall the story. A master before setting out on a journey entrusted varying numbers of talents (then a unit of money, but now a person's total personal resource) to certain persons to manage until his return. Upon his return, he called each servant for an account of managership. He rejoiced and rewarded those who managed responsibly but punished the one who did not.

It's rather hard to miss the message of that parable, that each of us is a responsible, accountable manager!

In mid-life each of us is manager of many things:

—a frail mortal body, which properly cared for may last longer and be much more effective.

—500 to 700 skills (remember?), including some vital ones that have not been recognized, discovered, or used.

—relationships with a number of people.

—values, goals, dreams, and beliefs that we have absorbed deeply into our being.

—positions of responsibility and leadership, where our actions and statements about these values and beliefs will be heard.

We have the rest of our lives to manage before God!

Somehow a middle-ager's theological self-understanding needs to bounce back and forth between the *pilgrim* image (where there is movement, insecurity, uncertainty, and change) and the *manager* image (where there is great responsibility, accountability, and opportunity). Both images apply to mid-life in a significant way. However, it is not clear to me how you put them together. (At first I tried combining them in a single image, but that just didn't work!)

Fourth, *a theology of middle age is a theology of new birth and becoming.* Iris Sangiuliano quotes the late poet Anne Sexton, "women are *born twice.*" Some are. Anne Sexton was one who was. She had never attended college but, instead, was the "little wife." Then one day she happened to hear some poetry. She thought, "I think I can do that!" And she did—her second birth.[8] Sangiuliano's study traces the path that women have taken toward a *second birth.* By this she means the emergence of an identity, a dream, a task that truly expresses who that woman is. It is the dawning of that separate distinct identity, being something other than someone's wife or someone's mother.

I am amazed that Sangiuliano uses this term "second birth" seemingly unconscious that she is using a Bible image. (Indeed, the term "born again" has been overused, abused, and made into a cliché by the media as they have attempted to understand the religious commitment of President Carter.) Sangiuliano uses the term "second birth" in a secular way, and yet what she describes has some important similarities to the biblical term "rebirth."

The basic biblical reference to rebirth is John, the third chapter, when Jesus tells Nicodemus, a mature, highly respected leader, ". . . unless one is born anew, he cannot see the kingdom of God" (John 3:3). William Barclay tells us the term translated "again" (*anōthen*) in this verse has three different meanings. It can mean: (1) from the beginning and, therefore, completely or radically; (2) again, for the second time; (3) from above, and, therefore, from God. Barclay suggests all three meanings are applicable in this Bible passage, which makes the phrase "born again" untranslatable in a single term. Instead, Barclay offers a whole sentence:

> To be born again is to undergo such a radical change that it is like a new birth; it is to have something happen to the soul which can only be described as being born all over again; and the whole process is not human achievement, because it comes from the grace and the power of God.[9]

Somehow Barclay's understanding of what that phrase "born again" means is of great help to me, for it pulls two seemingly quite different experiences together. The two experiences are: the experience of committing one's life to Jesus Christ and the experience of changing radically, discovering new possibilities within self, expressing vital new creativity. Both are second births, since they are both radical changes whose source is (from my faith perspective) Creator-Redeemer, God.

If you live and work with middle-aged people and have eyes to see, there is no doubt about it: Many middle-agers are getting in touch with new vital creative juices. They are being reborn and becoming in myriads of ways. Radical "new birth" is not just a doctrine but a vital personal experience. The slogan of these changed and changing persons is: "Please be patient. God is not finished with me yet." Their theme verse could be that assurance from Paul to a little congregation he had so loved and enjoyed, "And I am sure that he who began a good work in you will bring it to completion at the day of Jesus Christ" (Philippians 1:6).

Fifth, *a theology of middle age is a theology of grace.*

Again, Ken Mitchell writes:

> The theology appropriate to a middle-aged person is a theology which recognizes plainly and with considerable joy the freedom that comes in knowing that whatever we do will not save us. I am convinced that childhood and adolescence and young adulthood are all deeply touched by works righteousness, as if we could, by using all our gifts, buy time and save ourselves and defer any thought of there being a limit.[10]

Ken Mitchell is correct in a vital way. Middle age is a time when we may begin to shed some of those arrogant idolatries of self, such as "I know things and have abilities so I will accomplish more than anyone else has," or "The church (or school, or business, or whatever) was pretty irrelevant before I came along, but I can bring it around," etc.

Instead, the person in middle age may begin to experience the "paradox of grace." That is, if you accomplish something worthwhile, you sense it is because of God's grace working in you. If you fail, you have more peace, sensing that your justification by God depends on grace, not on achievement. You can look at your own finitude with increasing peace, for you sense the grace that touches you within life will also touch you at the end of it.

But this insight does not come easily. It comes only after living and struggling long enough that the inadequacy of any other view begins to come clear.

In 2 Corinthians 12, Paul tells of an experience that for me has become a parable of mid-life. He tells of a person (obviously himself) who was granted glorious visions and revelations of the Lord. These visions gave him a sense of triumph and certainty. Then when he might have become "too elated" by all this, "a thorn was given me in the flesh, a messenger of Satan. . . ."

I don't know what Paul's thorn was, but I know what mine is. My thorn is middle age, the egotistic dreams I will never achieve, the worthwhile tasks I will not finish, the daughters who will soon leave me, the increased probabilities of sickness, the certainty of death, the uncomfortable new searching I have to do.

Paul didn't like his thorn any better than I like mine. Three times he asked the Lord to take it away. Instead, the Lord gave him a perspective on that thorn. The Lord said, "My *grace* is sufficient for you, for my power is made perfect in weakness."

And Paul obediently (much more obediently than I, so far) concludes, "I will all the more gladly boast of my weaknesses, that the power of Christ may rest upon me . . . for when I am weak, then I am strong" (2 Corinthians 12:9*b*-10).

Sixth, *a theology of middle age is a theology of fellowship.*

In mid-life, some of us become more capable of entering into sustaining human community with each other. We men may shed some of our macho intensity, our competitiveness, our tendency to use people rather than relate to them. We discover more of our tender, caring side. Women may discover good things within themselves to share and to discover in community with others.

But in mid-life, some of us need that vital circle of caring people all the more as well. Our families shrink as our children leave, and our surviving parents may age or die. The loneliness of entering an era where we don't know all the answers haunts us. Our frailty frightens us. We need support.

Paul E. Johnson told of a friend who admitted the need for such community and so they formed a prayer group. For years this prayer community has gone on, where "in regular group meetings we have shared our deepest joys and sorrows, our hopes and fears, our doubts and faith." His friend described the meaning of this group in the following manner:

> All my life I have wanted to live in a community of "caring" people. This was apparent to you when I asked our Prayer Group to become such a

community. You were the kind of people on whom I could count to come to my rescue when my spirit was low and the storm loud, and the night dark, and the soul was sad and the heart oppressed. I could depend upon you to bring me strength in my hour of need so that I could be secure within your love, until I learned to sing God's song alone in the night. . . .

To my surprise and great joy, I found that being concerned with and involved in the despairing needs of those around me, and those far off as well, I was no longer so afraid and anxious about my own problems and needs. In fact to my utter amazement, I find them being taken care of, so much so that even my greatest worry, one that has continually troubled me day and night for the past thirty-one years is now being solved to my satisfaction and blessing. I am at peace day and night.[11]

As we move from the dependence of childhood to the independence of youth and young adult years, to the interdependence of middle adult years, we are open to just such experiences.

Our Bible tells us that our God has anticipated such needs and has created *koinonia*—fellowship, where human caring is the vehicle by which divine love is experienced. The intentional Christian community becomes the place where the cry of loneliness can be met with divine human koinonia. (It should be added that sometimes koinonia describes direct fellowship with Christ without the intervening community.)

It is delightful news to know we don't have to be pilgrims, managers-stewards, becomers, by ourselves. We are offered the opportunity to experience these things in a rich community of faith wherein God is present to love and to support.

These six elements, seen in some relationship to each other, are a beginning theology of middle age as I have experienced and reflected upon it. I suppose there should be some priority among these elements, but I am not sure what that priority would be. I only know that at times during the last five years each of these elements was vitally important to me in my mid-life needs. A theology of middle age would have a serious gap without any one of them. So for the present, see them as different facets of the same gem, which is still in rough stage and not at all finely polished. But there is one more element.

Seventh, *a theology of middle age is a theology of hope.*

Generally, biblical hope is that God's cosmic purposes will ultimately be worked out. As it touches the middle-ager's personal pilgrimage, hope is expressed in two ways.

First, there is hope to help me more frankly face the fact of my own death. The hope is that the God who has gone with me through life awaits me at the end in a manner that will be better than anything I have yet known. Again, Paul expresses the middle-ager's hope:

> . . . we do not lose heart. Though our outer nature is wasting away, our inner nature is being renewed every day. For this slight momentary affliction is preparing for us an eternal weight of glory beyond all comparison, because we look not to the things that are seen but to the things that are unseen; for the things that are seen are transient, but the things that are unseen are eternal.
>
> For we know that if the earthly tent we live in is destroyed, we have a building from God, a house not made with hands, eternal in the heavens (2 Corinthians 4:16–5:1).

> "'Death is swallowed up in victory.'
> 'O death, where is thy victory?
> O death, where is thy sting?' . . .

"But thanks be to God, who gives us the victory through our Lord Jesus Christ" (1 Corinthians 15:55, 57).

"Therefore, my beloved brethren, be steadfast, immovable, always abounding in the work of the Lord, knowing that in the Lord your labor is not in vain" (1 Corinthians 15:58).

But there is still another dimension to our hope. Like the psalmist:

> "I believe that I shall see the goodness of the Lord
> in the land of the living!"
>
> —Psalm 27:13

Whatever my present mood or situation (and there are some depressing, troubled periods in mid-life), I hope to know times of celebration, rejoicing, peace, and creativity again in my life. And the God of hope holds before me that possibility as well.

I was deeply touched by Paul E. Johnson's telling the story of Ludwig van Beethoven. A promising young piano virtuoso and composer, he discovered he was going deaf. At first he tried to conceal the affliction but eventually gave up playing the piano in public and cut himself off from all but his most intimate friends. He poured out his anguish in 1802:

> For me there can be no recreation in the society of my fellows, refined intercourse, mutual exchange of thought. I must live like an exile. . . .

O Providence—grant me at last but one day of pure joy—it is so long since really joy echoed in my heart—O when—O when, Divine One—shall I feel it again in the temple of nature and man—Never? No—O that would be too hard.[12]

The "deafness sent Beethoven to composing music with a passion he had not known before." He sought communion with the spirit and the solace of nature. Though he could not hear music anymore, he tried to "capture the majestic and turbulent chords he heard within." He composed a series of masterpieces in rapid succession.[13]

After a decade he entered a period of quiescence.

Then from 1818 to 1824, the giant stirred again. Beethoven's later works were pervaded with a spiritual radiance that reached a climax in the "Hymn to Joy" of the Ninth Symphony. Here as never before his struggle with sorrow and adversity came to fruition in joy, and his vision of brotherhood of all mankind in a feeling of dedication to humanity.

In no other symphony had he voiced such an all-encompassing mood of humanity, spirituality, and exaltation. Without his affliction and the pain of his struggle to overcome it, there would never have been the joy of creative life rising as a fountain to overflow to others.[14]

You and I are not Beethovens. But we may have parallel experiences. Out of our suffering, we have reason to believe that good things will happen again. What is the reason? Our God of hope.

    Middle-agers are beautiful!
        aren't we, Lord?
    I feel for us
        too radical for our parents
        too reactionary for our kids

        supposedly in the prime of life
          like prime rib
          everybody eating off me
            devouring me
          nobody thanking me
            appreciating me

        but still hanging in there
          communicating with my parents
          in touch with my kids

        and getting more in touch

with myself
and that's all good
thanks for making it good,
and
could you make it a little better?[15]

NOTES AND RESOURCES
FOR FURTHER EXPLORATION

Chapter 1
My Strange, Predictable Dis-Ease
Mid-Life Experienced

[1] Virginia Pipe. Personally prepared statement. Used with permission.

Chapter 2
Seasons, Passages, and Transformations
The Discovery of Middle Age

[1] Linda Wolfe, "The Dynamics of Personal Growth," *House and Garden*, vol. 148, no. 5 (May, 1976), p. 160.

[2] Quoted by Vivian Rogers McCoy, Colleen Ryan, and James W. Lichtenberg, *The Adult Life Cycle* (Lawrence, Kansas: Adult Life Center, Division of Continuing Education), p. 6.

[3] *Ibid.*

[4] Erik H. Erikson, *Childhood and Society* (New York: W. W. Norton & Co., Inc., 1950), pp. 247-273.

[5] William Bridges, *The Season of Our Lives* (Rolling Hills Estates, Calif.: Wayfarer Press, 1977), pp. 12-13.

[6] Daniel J. Levinson, Charlotte N. Darrow, Edward B. Klein, Maria H. Levinson, Braxton McKee, *The Seasons of a Man's Life* (New York: Alfred A. Knopf, Inc., 1978).

[7] *Ibid.,* p. 18.

[8] *Ibid.,* p. 19.

[9] *Ibid.,* pp. 56-62. These periods in adult development are taken from Daniel Levinson et al.

[10] *Ibid.,* p. 192.

[11] *Ibid.,* p. 61.

[12] *Ibid.,* pp. 330-336. These three aspects of the developmental work of early and middle adulthood are taken from Levinson et al.

[13] *Ibid.,* p. 333.

[14] Roger L. Gould, *Transformations* (New York: Simon & Schuster, Inc., 1978), p. 14.

[15] *Ibid.,* p. 18.

[16] *Ibid.,* p. 22.

[17] *Ibid.,* p. 24.

[18] *Ibid.,* p. 25.

[19] *Ibid.*, p. 39.

[20] *Ibid.*, p. 40.

[21] Gail Sheehy, *Passages* (New York: E. P. Dutton and Elsevier Book Operations, 1976). Copyright © 1974, 1976 by Gail Sheehy. Reprinted by permission of the publisher, E. P. Dutton.

[22] Iris Sangiuliano, *In Her Time* (New York: William Morrow & Co., Inc., 1978), p. 20.

[23] *Ibid.*, pp. 23-24.

[24] *Ibid.*, p. 304.

[25] *Ibid.*, pp. 159-160.

[26] *Ibid.*, p. 158.

[27] Eda LeShan, *The Wonderful Crisis of Middle Age* (New York: David McKay Co., Inc., Warner Books edition, 1973), p. 15.

[28] Jill Tweedie, "The Ages of Man—and Woman," *Saturday Review*, May 15, 1976, p. 31.

Chapter 3
Confronted with the Arithmetic of Life
Facing My Own Finitude

[1] Gail Sheehy, *Passages* (New York: E. P. Dutton and Elsevier Book Operations, 1974), p. 2. Copyright © 1974, 1976 by Gail Sheehy. Reprinted by permission of the publisher, E. P. Dutton.

[2] *Ibid.*, p. 4.

[3] *Ibid.*

[4] *Ibid.*, pp. 5-9.

[5] *Ibid.*, p. 8.

[6] Ernest Becker, *The Denial of Death* (New York: The Free Press, A Division of Macmillan Publishing Co., Inc., 1973), p. 215.

[7] *Ibid.*, p. ix.

[8] *Ibid.*, p. 26.

[9] *Ibid.*, p. 27.

[10] Elisabeth Kübler-Ross, *On Death and Dying* (New York: Macmillan, Inc., 1969), p. 141.

[11] *Ibid.*, p. 39.

[12] J. William Worden and William Proctor, *Personal Death Awareness* (Englewood Cliffs, N.J.: Prentice-Hall, Inc., 1976), pp. 11-13.

[13] *Ibid.*, pp. 13-16.

[14] *Ibid.*, p. 17.

[15] Kübler-Ross, *op. cit.*, pp. 38-137. These stages are succinctly stated in her book, *Death, the Final Stage of Growth* (Englewood Cliffs, N.J.: Prentice-Hall, Inc., 1975), p. 10.

[16] Kübler-Ross, *Death, the Final Stage of Growth*, p. 10.

[17] *Ibid.*, p. 161.

[18] Robert Jay Lifton and Eric Olson, *Living and Dying* (New York: Praeger Publishers, Inc., 1974), p. 77.

[19] *Ibid.*, p. 82. The previous has been a summary of pp. 69-82.

[20] Kübler-Ross, *Death, the Final Stage of Growth*, pp. 36-37.

[21] Quoted by Worden and Proctor, *op. cit.*, p. 69.

[22] Kübler-Ross, *Death, the Final Stage of Growth*, p. 166.

[23] *Ibid.*, p. 167.

Chapter 4
Do You Want to Be Whole?
Health Management for the Middle Adult

[1] *Bostonia*, vol. 52, no. 1 (Winter, 1978), p. 1. Published by the Office of Public Relations of Boston University.

[2] Dr. William Barclay, quoted in Peter Chew, *The Inner World of the Middle-Aged Man* (New York: Macmillan, Inc., 1976), p. 102.

[3] Quoted in Chew, *op. cit.*, p. 112.

[4] *Bostonia*, Winter, 1978, pp. 1-9.

[5] *Ibid.*, p. 9.

[6] *Ibid.*, p. 11.

[7] *Ibid.*, p. 12.

[8] *Ibid.*

[9] *Ibid.*, p. 14.

[10] Dr. Friedman, cited in Nancy Mayer, *The Male Mid-Life Crisis* (New York: Doubleday & Co., Inc., 1978), pp. 244-245.

[11] Bostonia, *op. cit.*, p. 15.

[12] *Ibid.*

[13] American Cancer Society undated pamphlets, "Safeguards Against Cancer" and "The Hopeful Side of Cancer."

[14] Eda LeShan, *The Wonderful Crisis of Middle Age* (New York: David McKay Co., Inc., Warner Books edition, 1973), pp. 243-245.

[15] *Blue Print for Health*, vol. 25, no. 1, entitled "Stress," p. 2. Published by the Blue Cross Association, 840 North Lake Shore Drive, Chicago, IL 60611.

[16] Dr. Donald Oken, "Stress . . . Our Friend, Our Foe," in *ibid.*, pp. 5-17.

[17] *Ibid.*, p. 15.

[18] *Ibid.*, p. 16.

[19] L. Robert Keck, *The Spirit of Synergy* (Nashville: Abingdon Press, 1978), p. 58.

[20] O. Carl Simonton and Stephanie Matthews-Simonton, "Belief Systems and Management of Emotional Aspects of Malignancy," *The Journal of Transpersonal Psychology*, 1975, no. 1, p. 38, quoted in Keck, *op. cit.*, p. 59.

[21] *Ibid.*

[22] Dr. Thomas H. Holmes and Dr. T. Stephenson Holmes, "How Change Can Make Us Ill," *Blue Print for Health*, pp. 66-75.

[23] *Ibid.* See p. 71 for the complete list.

[24] *Ibid.*, p. 73.

[25] Virginia Pipe, unpublished paper.

[29] Keck, *op. cit.*

Chapter 5
What Are You Going to Do, Now That You Are Growing Up?
Life Planning in the Mid-Years

[1] Gail Sheehy, *Passages* (New York: E. P. Dutton and Elsevier Book Operations, 1976), pp. 177-203. Copyright © 1974, 1976 by Gail Sheehy. Reprinted by permission of the publisher, E. P. Dutton.

[2] *Ibid.*, pp. 206-240.

[3] *Ibid.*, p. 16.

[4] Vivian Rogers McCoy, Carol Nalbandian, and Colleen Ryan, *Create: A New Model for Career Change* (Lawrence, Kansas: Adult Life Resource Center, The University of Kansas, 1979), p. 6.

⁵ Ray W. Ragsdale, *The Mid-Life Crisis of a Minister* (Waco, Texas: Word, Inc., 1978), pp. 48-53.

⁶ Virginia Pipe. Personally prepared material. Used by permission. Watch for the soon-to-be published book, "Menopause Is Not the Cause" in which Virginia and Mary Lou Reed will explore in depth the role of the homemaker in mid-life. Incidentally, similar courses to the one described are offered through women's programs of many community colleges or vocational-technical schools.

⁷ Richard Nelson Bolles, *What Color Is Your Parachute? A Practical Manual for Job-Hunters and Career Changers,* 1978 Revised Edition (Berkeley, Calif.: Ten Speed Press, 1978), preface. Copyright 1972, 1975, 1976, 1977, 1978 by Richard N. Bolles. Used by special permission. Those desiring a copy of the complete book for further reading may procure it from the publisher, Ten Speed Press, P. O. Box 7123, Berkeley CA 94707.

⁸ "Choosing a Second Career," *Business Week,* September 19, 1977.

⁹ If you request them, the National Career Development Project, P.O. Box 379, Walnut Creek, CA 94596 will send you the names of life career workshop leaders who have taken their training and live in your area. Possibly extension departments of state universities, local colleges, or vocational-technical schools may offer life-planning courses.

¹⁰ Richard Bolles, *The Quick Job-Hunting Map, Advanced Version* (Berkeley, Calif.: Ten Speed Press, 1975), pp. 2-3. Copyright 1975 by Richard N. Bolles and the National Career Development Project. Used by special permission. Those desiring a copy of the complete book for further reading may procure it from the publisher, Ten Speed Press, P. O. Box 7123, Berkeley, CA 94707.

¹¹ Richard Bolles, *The Three Boxes of Life and How to Get Out of Them* (Berkeley, Calif.: Ten Speed Press, 1978), pp. 138-139. Used by special permission. Those desiring a copy for further reading may procure it from the publisher, Ten Speed Press, P. O. Box 7123, Berkeley, CA 94707.

¹² *Ibid.,* pp. 142-155.

¹³ Bolles, *The Quick Job-Hunting Map,* pp. 18-19.

¹⁴ This material has been an outline of Richard Bolles's method of life planning. It is given in brief outline in *The Quick Job-Hunting Map* and in more detail in *What Color Is Your Parachute?* (both cited above).

¹⁵ Bolles, *What Color Is Your Parachute?,* pp. 88-89.

¹⁶ Refer to Herbert J. Freudenberger, "Staff Burn-out," *Journal of Social Issues,* vol. 30, no. 1 (1974), pp. 159-165, and Christina Maslach, "Burned-Out," *Human Behavior,* September, 1976, pp. 16-22.

Chapter 6
The Toughest Challenge of the Middle Years
Marriage for Middle-Agers

¹ Eda LeShan, *The Wonderful Crisis of Middle Age* (New York: David McKay Co., Inc., Warner Books edition, 1973), p. 143.

² Howard J. Clinebell, Jr., *Growth Counseling for Mid-Years Couples* (Philadelphia: Fortress Press, 1977), p. 22.

³ *U. S. News and World Report,* December 20, 1976, p. 56.

⁴ Robert O. Blood, Jr., and Donald M. Wolfe, *Husbands & Wives* (New York: The Free Press, 1960), p. 264.

⁵ Robert Lee and Marjorie Casebier, *The Spouse Gap* (Nashville: Abingdon Press, 1971), pp. 164-165.

[6] George R. Bach and Peter Wyden, *The Intimate Enemy* (New York: William Morrow & Co., Inc., 1969).

[7] Clayton C. Barbeau, *Creative Marriage: The Middle Years* (New York: The Seabury Press, Inc., 1976), p. 63.

[8] Gail Sheehy, "The Crisis Couples Face at 40," *McCalls,* vol. 103, no. 8 (May, 1976), pp. 157, 159.

[9] *Ibid.,* p. 159.

[10] *Ibid.*

[11] James A. Peterson, *Married Love in the Middle Years* (Wilton, Conn.: Association Press, 1968), p. 38.

[12] Barbara Fried, *The Middle-Age Crisis* (New York: Harper & Row, Publishers, Inc., 1967), p. 102.

[13] Quoted in Lee and Casebier, *op. cit.,* pp. 82-83.

[14] *Ibid.,* p. 83.

[15] Nancy Mayer, *The Male Mid-Life Crisis* (New York: Doubleday & Co., Inc., 1978), p. 219.

[16] Lee and Casebier, *op. cit.,* pp. 99-100.

[17] Barbeau, *op. cit.,* p. 61.

[18] Peterson, *op. cit.,* pp. 54-58.

[19] Barbeau, *op. cit.,* p. 77.

[20] Two organizations that can put you in touch with groups for enriching marriage are: Association of Couples for Marriage Enrichment, P.O. Box 10596, Winston-Salem, NC 27108; and Interpersonal Communications Program, Inc., 300 Clifton Ave., Minneapolis, MN 55403. In addition to the books I have already mentioned, I commend to you *Friends, Partners, and Lovers* by Warren Lane Molton (Valley Forge: Judson Press, 1979).

Chapter 7
Singleness and Remarriage
Alternative Life-Styles for Middle-Agers

[1] Adeline McConnell and Beverly Anderson, *Single After Fifty* (New York: McGraw-Hill Book Company, 1978), p. 2. Used by permission of McGraw-Hill Book Company. In the following pages I will be summarizing their outline of experience which coincides with my counseling experience and observation in many ways.

[2] *Ibid.,* p. 19.

[3] *Ibid.,* p. 285.

[4] *Ibid.*

[5] *Ibid.,* pp. 289-290.

[6] Brenda Maddox, *The Half-Parent* (New York: A Signet Book, New American Library, 1975), pp. 7-9.

[7] Ruth Roosevelt and Jeannette Lofas, *Living in Step* (New York: McGraw-Hill Book Company, 1976), p. 19.

[8] Mel Krantzler, *Learning to Love Again* (New York: Thomas Y. Crowell Company, Publishers, 1977), p. 219.

[9] Maddox, *op. cit.,* p. 29.

[10] Roosevelt and Lofas, *op. cit.,* pp. 54-55.

[11] *Ibid.,* p. 56.

[12] *Ibid.,* pp. 85-86.

[13] Krantzler, *op. cit.,* pp. 236-243.

[14] Myrna and Robert Kysar, *The Asundered* (Atlanta: John Knox Press, 1978), p. 104.

Chapter 8
The Middle Generation
The Mid-Life Person As Parent and Child

[1] Erma Bombeck, *If Life Is a Bowl of Cherries, What Am I Doing in the Pits?* (New York: McGraw-Hill Book Company, 1971, 1972, 1973, 1974, 1975, 1976, 1977, 1978), pp. 195-196. Quoted with permission.

[2] Evelyn Millis Duvall, *Family Development* (Philadelphia: J. B. Lippincott Company, 1957), pp. 294-297.

[3] Haim G. Ginott, *Between Parent and Teenager* (New York: Macmillan, Inc., 1969), pp. 25-26.

[4] *Ibid.*, p.25.

[5] *Ibid.*, p. 28.

[6] Anna Freud, "Adolescence," in *The Psychoanalytic Study of the Child* (New York: International University Press, 1958). quoted in *ibid.*, p. 29.

[7] Kenneth Keniston and the Carnegie Council on Children, *All Our Children* (New York: Harcourt Brace Jovanovich, Inc., 1977), pp. 8-9.

[8] *Ibid.*, p. 17.

[9] *Ibid.*, p. 18.

[10] *Ibid.*

[11] Margaret Mead, *Culture and Commitment* (New York: Natural History Press/Doubleday & Co., Inc., 1970).

[12] Here are some good books to read and discuss on this subject: Thomas Gordon, *Parent Effectiveness Training* (New York: Wyden Books, 1970). Shirley Gould, *Teenagers, the Continuing Challenge* (New York: Hawthorn Books, Inc., 1977). Paul Welter, *Family Problems and Predicaments: How to Respond* (Wheaton: Tyndale House Publishers, 1977).

[13] Bombeck, *op. cit.*, pp. 184-189. Quoted with permission.

[14] Barbara Silverstone and Helen Kandel Hyman, *You and Your Aging Parent* (New York: Pantheon Books, Inc., 1976), p. 11. Another good resource for this subject is: Jane Otten and Florence D. Shelley, *When Your Parents Grow Old* (New York: Funk & Wagnalls, Inc., 1976).

Chapter 9
Shifting into Growth
The Inward Journey

[1] Nena and George O'Neill, *Shifting Gears* (New York: Avon Books, 1974). Copyright © 1974 by Nena O'Neill and George O'Neill. Reprinted by permission of the publisher, M. Evans and Company, Inc., New York, New York 10017.

[2] *Ibid.*, pp. 48-51.

[3] *Ibid.*, p. 54.

[4] *Ibid.*, p. 61.

[5] *Ibid.*, p.62.

[6] Peter Chew, *The Inner World of the Middle-Aged Man* (New York: Macmillan, Inc., 1976), p. 5.

[7] Carl Gustav Jung, quoted by Howard Clinebell, *Growth and Counseling for Mid-Years Couples* (Philadelphia: Fortress Press, 1977), p. 40.

[8] Henry C. Simmons, "The Quiet Journey: Psychological Development and Religious Growth from Ages Thirty to Sixty," *Religious Education,* vol. 71, no. 2

(March-April, 1976), p. 133. Quoted by permission of the publisher, the Religious Education Association, 409 Prospect Street, New Haven, CT 06510. Membership subscription available for $20.00 per year.

[9] *Ibid.*, p. 134.

[10] Clinebell, *op. cit.*, pp. 41–42.

[11] Simmons, *op. cit.*, p. 141.

[12] *Ibid.*

[13] John H. Westerhoff III, *Will Our Children Have Faith?* (New York: The Seabury Press, Inc., 1976), p. 39; see also pp. 89–99.

[14] Daniel Levinson, Charlotte N. Darrow, Edward B. Klein, Maria H. Levinson, Braxton McKee, *The Seasons of a Man's Life* (New York: Alfred A. Knopf, Inc., 1978), p. 335.

[15] Nena and George O'Neill, *op. cit.*, pp. 218–219.

[16] Quoted from a speech given by Howard Clinebell at the Convocation on Preaching and the American Revolution, at Providence, Rhode Island, September, 1976.

[17] Dr. Nathan W. Shock, quoted in Reuel Howe, *How to Stay Younger While Growing Older* (Waco, Texas: Word, Inc., 1974), p. 19.

[18] *Ibid.*, pp. 18–19.

[19] Florida Scott-Maxwell, quoted in Henri J. M. Nouwen and Walter Gaffney, *Aging* (New York: Doubleday & Co., Inc., 1974), p. 63.

[20] Bernice Neugarten, "The Psychology of Aging," in *The Adult Life Cycle* by Vivian Rogers McCoy, Colleen Ryan, and James W. Lichtenberg (Lawrence, Kansas: Adult Life Resource Center, University of Kansas, 1978), p. 240.

[21] David Ray, "Ten Rules for Retirement Preparation," *The Forty Plus Handbook* (Waco, Texas: Word, Inc., 1979), pp. 11–34; used by permission of WORD BOOKS, PUBLISHER, Waco, Texas 76703.

[22] Personal conversation with Virginia Pipe. Used by permission.

[23] From "A Living Will," prepared by the Euthanasia Education Council, 250 West 57th Street, New York, NY 10019, quoted in *Maggie Kuhn on Aging,* A Dialogue, edited by Dieter Hessel (Philadelphia: The Westminster Press, 1977), p. 111.

Chapter 10
Shifting into Growth (continued)
The Outward Journey

[1] James Sloan Allen, "I Want to Be As Much of Me As I Can Be," *The Nation*, vol. 226, no. 17 (May 6, 1978), p. 546.

[2] Tom Wolfe, "The 'ME' Decade and the Third Great Awakening," *New York,* August 23, 1976, p. 36. Reprinted by permission of International Creative Management. © 1976 by Tom Wolfe.

[3] *Ibid.*, p. 40.

[4] Daniel J. Levinson et al, *The Seasons of a Man's Life* (New York: Alfred A. Knopf, Inc., 1978), p. 242.

[5] Lawrence Kohlberg, "Moral Stages and Moralization," in Thomas Lickona, *Moral Development and Behavior* (New York: Holt, Rinehart & Winston, 1976), pp. 34–35.

[6] *Ibid.*, p. 33.

[7] Adam Daniel Finnerty, *No More Plastic Jesus* (Maryknoll, N.Y.: Orbis Books, 1977), p. 97.

Chapter 11
The Destruction That Wastes at Noonday
A Theology of Middle Age

[1] Elliot Jacques, "Death and the Mid-Life Crisis," *International Journal of Psychoanalysis,* vol. 46, 1965, p. 506.

[2] George W. Forell, *The Protestant Faith* (Englewood Cliffs, N.J.: Prentice-Hall, Inc., 1960), p. 116.

[3] *Ibid.,* p. 117.

[4] Dr. Kenneth Mitchell, quoted in "The Death of a Parent: Its Impact on Middle-Aged Sons and Daughters," personally distributed essay by Herbert Anderson, Wartburg Seminary, Dubuque, Iowa.

[5] Herbert Anderson, "The Death of a Parent: Its Impact on Middle-Aged Sons and Daughters," personally distributed essay, Wartburg Seminary, Dubuque, Iowa.

[6] Perceptive biblical theologians may be concerned that death is here viewed as part of God's providence. Does not the Bible also state a connection between sin and death, most graphically in Romans 5:12? What about death as a consequence of sin—or at least intimately connected to sin?

Paul Tillich (*Shaking of the Foundations* [New York: Charles Scribner's Sons, 1948], p. 70) points out that two things exist at the same time: "We have to die, because we are dust. That is the law of nature. . . . But, at the same time, we have to die because we are guilty. That is the moral law. . . ."

What is the connection between sin and death? Old Testament writers saw them both as barriers to the person's vital contact with God and, therefore, integrally related.

In the New Testament, the term "death" is used in at least three different ways: (*a*) to be a sinner cut off from vital contact with God; (*b*) to leave (die to) that life and enter into life with Christ (Romans 6:2-11); (*c*) physical death. And so the invitation is to die (definition *b*) to death (definition *a*) so that death (definition *c*) is not the end of all.

I have written the section on providence assuming that death (definition *c*) was in the providence of God who gave us death (definition *b*) as a means to triumph over and cope with physical death (definition *c*).

[7] Robert Raines, "The Second Half of Life," *Faith at Work,* vol. 89, no. 3 (April, 1976), p. 11.

[8] Iris Sangiuliano, *In Her Time* (New York: William Morrow & Co., Inc., 1978), p. 19.

[9] William Barclay, *The Gospel of John* (Edinburgh: The Saint Andrew Press, 1956), vol. 1, pp. 113-114.

[10] Anderson, *op. cit.*

[11] Paul E. Johnson, *The Middle Years* (Philadelphia: Fortress Press, 1971), pp. 59-60. Reprinted by permission of Fortress Press.

[12] *Ibid.,* p. 22.

[13] *Ibid.*

[14] *Ibid.,* pp. 22-23.

[15] Robert A. Raines, *Lord, Could You Make It a Little Better?* (Waco, Texas: Word, Inc., 1972), p. 135. Used by permission of WORD BOOKS, PUBLISHER, Waco, Texas 76703.

Other books helpful in thinking through a theology of middle age include the following: John Claypool, *Stages* (Waco: Word, Inc., 1977); Gerald O. Colling, *The Second Journey* (New York: Paulist Press, 1978); Robert Raines, *Going Home* (San Francisco: Harper & Row, Publishers, Inc., 1979).

INDEX

INDEX OF BIBLE RESOURCES CITED